Troublemakers
in Trousers

Women and What They Wore
to Get Things Done

Trouble in

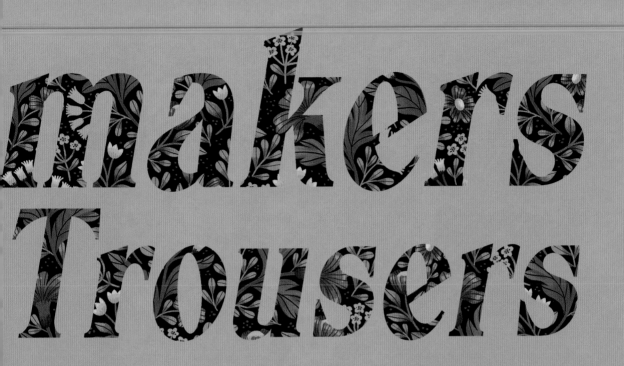

makers
Trousers

Women and What They Wore to Get Things Done

Sarah Albee

Illustrated by **Kaja Kajfež**

Charlesbridge

*For Cassie, Dara, Hannah, Isabel, May, and Sofia:
the next generation of troublemakers. Grandma Connie
would be proud.—S. A.*

*For my mum, the kindest and sweetest soul I know,
and for my grandmother, whose wisdom and humbleness
never cease to inspire me.—K. K.*

Published by Charlesbridge
9 Galen Street
Watertown, MA 02472
(617) 926-0329
www.charlesbridge.com

Printed in China
(hc) 10 9 8 7 6 5 4 3 2 1

Illustrations done in digital media
Display type set in Voska by Agung Gumilang Sugih,
    Yana by Laura Worthington, and ITC Goudy Sans
    by Frederic Goudy
Text type set in Chaparal Pro by Carol Twombly
Printed by 1010 Printing International Limited in Huizhou,
    Guangdong, China
Production supervision by Jennifer Most Delaney
Designed by Jon Simeon

Library of Congress Cataloging-in-Publication Data
Names: Albee, Sarah, author. | Kajfez, Kaja, illustrator.
Title: Troublemakers in trousers: Women and what they
    wore to get things done / Sarah Albee; Illustrated by
    Kaja Kajfež.
Description: Watertown: Charlesbridge, 2022. | Includes
    bibliographical references. | Audience: Ages 9–12 |
    Audience: Grades 4–6 | Summary: "Meet twenty-one
    women through history who wore men's clothing,
    pretended to be men, or broke the rules in order to do
    something they wanted—or needed—to do."—Provid-
    ed by publisher.
Identifiers: LCCN 2021013850 (print) | LCCN
    2021013851 (ebook) | ISBN 9781623540951 (hard-
    cover) | ISBN 9781632898531 (ebook)
Subjects: LCSH: Women—Attitudes—History—Juvenile
    literature. | Feminism—History—Juvenile literature.
    | Women—Biography—Juvenile literature.
Classification: LCC HQ1150 .A523 2022 (print) | LCC
    HQ1150 (ebook) | DDC 305.4209--dc23
LC record available at https://lccn.loc.gov/2021013850
LC ebook record available at https://lccn.loc.
    gov/2021013851

Table of Contents

Suit Yourself

What Not to Wear, Historically

Buckle up. You're about to embark on a series of adventures with some of the bravest real-life characters you'll ever meet. The lives of these twenty-one women were filled with adventure and peril and heroic courage. Some were queens. Some were pirates. Some were soldiers, or athletes, or outlaws. And although they lived at different times and in different places, there's one common thread that binds them. Each woman, at some point in her life, for one reason or another, put on breeches, armor, knickerbockers, a uniform, bloomers, pantaloons, buckskin pants, a three-piece suit, or trousers. And doing *that* was a "fashion don't" in most parts of the world, for most of history. In fact, before the twentieth century, so-called cross-dressing—women wearing men's clothes or men wearing women's clothes—was actually against the law.

As a result of what they wore and how they behaved, the women in this book endured serious backlash. It ranged from curious stares and hostile comments to being fined, arrested, or even executed.

What Exactly Are "Boy Clothes" and "Girl Clothes"?

Nowadays you have a lot more flexibility to dress in clothes that reflect your personality and style. But that probably wasn't the case for your grandparents or even your parents. The written and unwritten rules about what to wear have shifted over time and in many parts of the world.

 In ancient and medieval times, most men did not wear pants. They wore dress-like attire. Go ahead and call it a tunic, toga, loincloth, chiton, kilt, sarong, or robes. Whatever. Men did not wear pants. (In many countries today, men still don't.)

 During the European Renaissance (roughly 1400–1630), aristocratic men wore makeup, perfume, dangly earrings, and lacy shirts.

 Men were the first to wear high heels. Sure, the heels kept their boots in the stirrups when they rode a horse. But the heeled footwear was also fashionable. Women weren't that into shoes because for most of history, their skirts went down to the ground and hid their feet, so why bother?

 Everyone knows that pink is for girls and blue is for boys, right? Wrong. That's a modern, Western-world notion. An American publication from 1918 about infant wear stated: "The generally accepted rule is pink for the boys, and blue for the girls. The reason is that pink, being a more decided and stronger color, is more suitable for the boy, while blue, which is more delicate and dainty, is prettier for the girl."

 Up until the mid-twentieth century, most little boys in well-to-do European and American families sported shoulder-length, curly hair and flouncy dresses. At the age of six or seven, they got their first haircut and started wearing trousers.

A young boy in pink, about 1840.

Historic Fashion Fails

 In nineteenth-century America, twenty-one states passed laws that prohibited dressing in the clothing of the "opposite" gender.

 In the United States between 1910 and 1940, men were required to wear a skirt over their bathing trunks. Women's bathing suits could not be higher than six inches above the knee. Officials with rulers trawled beaches on the lookout for violators.

 In the 1960s a fashionable society woman walked into a posh New York restaurant dressed in the latest look—a pantsuit. She was stopped at the door because the restaurant's dress code didn't allow women to wear pants. So she stepped out of her trousers, handed them to her husband, and strolled to her table wearing only her thigh-length tunic top.

 In 1972 a civil-rights law called Title IX was passed. It stated, among other things, that schools receiving federal money could no longer require girls to wear dresses or skirts to school.

 In 1995 a judge in South Carolina refused to let a lawyer into his courtroom because she was wearing pants.

Who Is in This Book?

In many parts of the world, people have been divided into one of two genders: boy/man or girl/woman. But gender is a spectrum. Not everyone identifies as either a boy or a girl. And not everyone ends up identifying as the gender they were assigned when they were born.

From what the historical records suggest, the women in this book identified themselves as women. That's why I've used female pronouns (she/her) to describe them. But bear in mind that it's impossible to know for sure.

 Until a two-hundred-year-old law was revoked in 2013, women in Paris, France, could be arrested for wearing pants in public.

 In 2016 a Pennsylvania high-school girl was prevented from attending her prom because she was wearing a tuxedo instead of a dress.

 As recently as 2016 the Women's National Basketball Association (WNBA) offered first-year players classes in fashion, hair, and makeup tips. And in 2008 instruction in makeup and fashion took up nearly one-third of the league's two-day rookie-orientation program.

What Were They Thinking?

Some of the women you're about to meet disguised themselves as men. They did it to see the world, escape enslavement, fight for their country, flee from a horrible husband, or pursue a career closed to women.

Others didn't pretend they were men. They wore masculine clothing because it was more practical. Imagine trying to shoot an arrow while galloping bareback at fifty miles an hour toward an advancing enemy. Would you rather wear a shirt and buckskin trousers or a corset and hoopskirt? Imagine storming a castle while fending off poleaxes and

Twin brothers in the early 1600s.

flaming arrows. Would you rather be in a suit of armor or a long dress with sleeves so tight you can't raise your arms above your shoulders? Or imagine you're about to leap onto the slippery deck of an enemy ship and need to come up in a crouch, ready for battle. Would you want to wear loose sailor pants or a gown? You see the appeal.

Some women dressed like men just because they wanted to. They didn't care what people thought, and they were rich enough or royal enough that no one dared to tell them not to.

And finally, in the case of some women, history isn't a hundred percent sure about what kind of clothing they wore, because they belonged to cultures that passed information orally, from one generation to the next. So what they might have worn is subject to speculation. But they still belong in this book. These women defied convention and custom—sometimes even the law—and assumed nontraditional roles in order to accomplish their goals.

In this book you'll read the stories of twenty-one extraordinary women who dressed and acted as they did to get a job done. But the truth is, history is chockablock with amazing, trailblazing risk-takers—way more than can fit into one book. Here are a few more daring dressers whose stunning stories you might consider delving into: Dorothy Lawrence, James Barry, Zheng Shih, Sarah Emma Edmonds, Zora Neale Hurston, Queen Nyabingi, Albert Cashier, Josephine Baker, Charley Parkhurst, Mary Walker, Casimir Pulaski, Rose Pinon de Freycinet, and Mabel Mercer.

There are also many Scythian, Parthian, Persian, East Asian, South Asian, African, and Native American women who dared to dress and behave differently in order to accomplish great things and whose names, whether because of language barriers, lack of written documentation, or flat-out discrimination by historians, have receded into the mists of Western history. Maybe *you* can uncover their stories. Maybe you can tell those stories to the world.

Hatshepsut

ABOUT 1507 BCE TO ABOUT 1458 BCE

Girls Rule

The civilization of ancient Egypt thrived for three thousand years. To give you an idea of how long that is, at the time Hatshepsut (haht-SHEP-soot) became the king—called the pharaoh—the pyramids at Giza were already a thousand years old. Cleopatra wouldn't be born for another fourteen centuries.

Throughout the course of all those centuries, the lives of ordinary Egyptians didn't change much. Most people were peasant farmers who lived along the fertile banks of the Nile River, irrigating their fields and tending their crops. During summers, when the Nile River flooded its banks and submerged the land, people took time off from farming to build temples and pyramids for the pharaoh.

Ancient Egyptians also worshipped many gods. Everyone believed the pharaoh was the earthly link between gods and mortals. They also believed that the pharaoh was supposed to be a "he." Which made things tricky for Hatshepsut when she declared herself the new pharaoh, because she was a "she."

Hatshepsut's solution to anyone's concern was to wage a public-relations campaign showing statues and pictures of herself as a male pharaoh, complete with broad shoulders and a fake beard. She knew everyone knew she was female. But she also knew what ordinary Egyptians expected their pharaoh to look like. Most commoners never set eyes on the pharaoh. No matter what the pharaoh actually looked like (and many would never have won a beauty contest), every pharaoh's statues and pictures showed an idealized male figure with a muscular, broad-shouldered body. So Hatshepsut made sure hers did too.

During ancient Egypt's long history, there were only a handful of female pharaohs. Cleopatra is the most famous, but Hatshepsut was one of the greatest. How did she get to be the pharaoh in the first place?

The Emperor's New Clothes

Hatshepsut was born a princess. Her father was the pharaoh Thutmose I. Hatshepsut's dad fathered a son, Thutmose II, with one of his secondary wives. That meant that Thutmose II was Hatshepsut's half brother, and being a boy and all, he was the heir to the throne. When Hatshepsut was about twelve, she and Thutmose II got married. Egyptians didn't think it was weird for close family members to marry one another. They thought it was more important to keep royal bloodlines pure.

When Thutmose I died, Hatshepsut's husband/half brother, Thutmose II, became pharaoh as planned. That made Hatshepsut the queen. Images of them from this time show her standing obediently behind her husband.

After reigning for a few years, Hatshepsut's pharaoh-husband died unexpectedly. He'd fathered a son and heir, Thutmose III, with one of his lesser wives, but Thutmose III was much too young to be pharaoh. (He was probably only about two.) Someone needed to run Egypt. So Hatshepsut decided she'd do it. She became the regent, which is a grown-up who oversees a kingdom until the king is old enough to take over.

Pictures from this time show her as a woman, but not a typical woman. Women in Egyptian art are usually shown standing meekly behind their husbands or other male relatives. They wear long, narrow dresses and keep their feet close together and their arms at their sides. Hatshepsut, on the other hand, is seen striding confidently forward, with her arm outstretched. That was more of a traditional male stance, and it's a clue to her growing leadership role.

A few years into her reign as regent to the child-pharaoh, new images of Hatshepsut appeared, depicting her as a broad-shouldered king with a beard, standing next to Thutmose III rather than behind him. The two now looked like male corulers. It's likely that these new images were her idea.

It was about that time that Hatshepsut shipped Thutmose III off to a distant part of the kingdom. He was probably around seven or eight. Scholars used to think she did this to get rid of him so she could grab power for herself. But nowadays most historians believe that she intended to send him somewhere safe where he could grow to manhood and train to become a warrior.

Nevertheless, she was now the lone ruler of Egypt. In order to protect Thutmose III's position as next in line to rule, she probably felt she needed to justify her own status. So she invented a story about her divine birth. She declared that her true father was the god Amun, which made her a half god and legitimized her claim to become the pharaoh. And people bought it.

Reign Check

Hatshepsut did a lot of great things during her reign. She established relative peace and prosperity. She increased trade with Egypt's neighbors, shored up mining in the Sinai Desert, and ushered in a glorious period of art. She also really liked to build stuff.

Early pharaohs built huge pyramids for themselves, crammed full of treasure and items that they might need for the afterlife. But pyramids were easy targets for grave robbers and tomb raiders, who broke in and carried away everything that wasn't nailed down.

By the time of Hatshepsut's reign, pharaohs had stopped building pyramids. They began building their tombs underground in long, hidden tunnels. So while Hatshepsut didn't construct

Her Right-Hand Man

Hatshepsut became close to one of her advisors. His name was Senenmut. She appointed him as tutor to her young daughter and promoted him to the position of great steward of an important temple. Then she put him in charge of constructing her own temple. He also oversaw quarrying the stone for her obelisks. Each one had to be hacked from a single piece of granite and lugged on boats for hundreds of miles, which required perfect balance and a lot of mathematical calculations. One mistake could sink the whole thing, along with a lot of people.

As a token of her thanks, Hatshepsut presented him with a fancy sarcophagus, which is a stone box for your dead body. That might seem like an odd present to give someone, but not to an ancient Egyptian.

Up until pretty recently, historians assumed that Senenmut was Hatshepsut's boyfriend and the real power behind her throne. But they weren't giving Hatshepsut the credit she deserved. Senenmut may have pined for her privately, but she was definitely in charge.

Hatshepsut as a broad-shouldered male king, wearing a false beard and kilt.

any pyramids, she found plenty of other things to build. In Karnak, she adorned the entrance to one temple dedicated to Amun with colossal statues of herself, along with lions and sphinxes and carved hieroglyphics that told the story of her divine birth. Another entrance had a couple of hundred-foot, four-hundred-ton obelisks. Her supersize mortuary temple in Thebes, built at the base of some limestone cliffs on the west bank of the Nile, remains an architectural masterpiece. The message all these magnificent constructions sent was not lost on her subjects: your pharaoh might be female, but she is part god and all-powerful.

Stony Silence

Hatshepsut reigned for twenty-two years. Then Thutmose III returned, ready to take over as the next pharaoh. How did he feel about his aunt-stepmother? For a long time, Egyptologists believed that Thutmose III returned in a rage, furious at having been kicked off his throne for all that time. Those early (and male) historians were all too willing to paint Hatshepsut as a scheming female interloper who wrested the throne away from its rightful (male) heir. It's true that Thutmose III and some of his descendants would later destroy nearly all traces

of her reign. They came close to erasing her from the history books. Her statues were bashed to pieces and tossed into a big pit. Her monuments were defaced, and her cartouche, or name symbol, was chiseled out of walls. Thutmose III left her big temple alone, but he redecorated it with his own name.

But more recently historians have proposed a different theory. Many now believe that the destruction wasn't done in anger. They think Hatshepsut peacefully stepped aside when she became too old and allowed Thutmose III to take over. After she died, he performed all her funeral rites and was her chief mourner. He then waited twenty years into his reign before ordering the destruction. And it was only her kingly depictions that were trashed. He left her queenly images alone. If he were really that angry, he would have probably had all her images defaced. Nowadays scholars believe Thutmose III did what he did because he wanted to avoid upsetting the natural balance of things. He may have thought the idea of a female king would confuse common Egyptians. Also he probably didn't want future ambitious women to get any ideas. So he let history think she'd been merely a queen, and he erased her time as pharaoh. He even backdated his reign to the death of his father.

Hatshepsut's mortuary temple, an architectural masterpiece.

A Royal Missing-Person Case

In the past, researchers considered Hatshepsut a minor footnote in Egyptian history. No one knew where her burial tomb was. But after scholars cracked the key to reading Egyptian hieroglyphics, they realized that Hatshepsut had been more than a queen. She'd been a pharaoh. But where was she buried?

In 2007 a long-overlooked mummy that had been found back in 1903 in a random, unmarked tomb in the Valley of the Kings became a person of interest to archaeologists. Why? Well, first, it was clearly a woman. What was a female mummy doing in the Valley of the Kings? Up until that point, the only parts of Hatshepsut that archaeologists had found were her liver and a tooth. The ancient embalmer—the guy whose job it was to preserve a dead body for the afterlife—probably chucked the tooth in with the liver as an afterthought. It was a molar with part of its root missing.

Then an Egyptologist realized that in the jaw socket of the anonymous mummy, there was a root with no tooth. Hatshepsut's tooth fit the mummy's jaw socket. People now believe that the anonymous mummy is the remains of Hatshepsut.

Nowadays, thanks to CT scans, archaeologists can learn a lot more about mummies than they used to—including what the people looked like and how they died—without needing to unwrap them.

The real Hatshepsut bore little resemblance to her statues, which depicted a muscular, broad-shouldered man. She was a stout woman of about fifty when she died. Her fingernails were painted red and outlined in black. She had terrible teeth problems and may actually have died from an infected tooth—people did that in the days before modern dentistry. Or possibly she died from bone cancer or from slathering on too much face cream (which modern scientists have determined was probably toxic) for a skin condition.

Hatshepsut's name is now restored to the roster of rulers. Today she is recognized as one of the greatest Egyptian pharaohs who ever lived.

Hypsicratea

FIRST CENTURY BCE

A Groom of One's Own

Stories about the Amazons—the warrior women from Greek mythology—have been popular for thousands of years, and they still are. Modern-day fictional characters such as Mulan, Xena the Warrior Princess, and Wonder Woman have Amazon origins. But did Amazons really exist? You betcha. This is the story of one real-life Amazon princess.

Hypsicratea (hip-sih-kruh-TAY-uh) was a warrior who spent most of her life on the back of a horse. Both the ancient Greeks and the ancient Romans would have called her an Amazon. But then, those ancient male writers called *all* female warriors Amazons, and they were kind of obsessed with them. The idea that a woman could even *be* a warrior completely blew their minds. The Greeks would also have called her a barbarian, because that's what they called all the tribes of nomadic people who didn't speak Greek and who traveled around Central Asia on horseback.

We don't know much about Hypsicratea's girlhood or exactly where she came from. She was probably Persian or Scythian. She spent her youth trekking through the steep, snow-covered slopes of the Caucasus Mountains, which jut up between the Black Sea and the Caspian Sea in modern-day Russia and Georgia. Such a lifestyle would have made her tough as nails.

Hypsicratea enters the historical record about the time she and a few thousand of her tribespeople, both male and female, were recruited to join the army of King Mithradates of Pontus (part of ancient Turkey).

She cut her hair short, tugged on a tunic, and tucked her patterned trousers into her high boots. Plutarch, a historian from ancient times, wrote that she was "a girl always of a manly and daring spirit . . . attired and mounted like a Persian horseman."

Hypsicratea clearly stood out as an exceptional warrior on horseback in a culture that was *full* of exceptional warriors on horseback. Women archers could be as effective as men, so in Hypsicratea's world, men and women warriors played equal roles in battle.

A skilled archer could launch fifteen to twenty arrows a minute from the back of a galloping horse without stirrups, reins, or a saddle. The smaller Scythian-style bow was accurate and deadly at long distances, and because it was held away from the body to shoot, the rider could turn around in the saddle either to the right or to the left and shoot arrows backward at a full gallop—the so-called parting shot.

Impressed by her horsemanship, Mithradates promoted Hypsicratea to head groom, and as a show of affection

and respect, called her by the masculine form of her name, Hypsicrates. Then they seem to have legit fallen in love. She became his queen, and they became the power couple of the ancient world.

Mithradates

Hypsicratea's husband, Mithradates, would eventually rule ancient Greece and most of Turkey. The Romans hated him. During the first century BCE, Rome was growing all-powerful, and Greece was in decline. But Mithradates refused to yield to Roman rule, and his rebellious kingdom was a thorn in Rome's side. There's a whole period of ancient Roman history known as the Mithradatic Wars, a series of bloody clashes between the Romans and that cunning old king of Pontus.

Hypsicratea was probably Mithradates's sixth wife. He had multiple children with multiple concubines. No one would describe Mithradates as a warm and fuzzy guy. He had enemies who wanted him dead. But he also had allies from Central Asia all the way to Spain, united by a shared resentment toward Roman invaders.

Mithradates's soldiers fought fiercely, showing little mercy for those in their path. Their tactics included driving chariots with razor-sharp rotating blades, shooting arrows dipped in snake venom, and tricking enemy soldiers into eating poisonous honey. When Roman soldiers burrowed tunnels underground in hope of breaking through his ranks, Mithradates ordered his soldiers to lob nests of stinging hornets into the tunnels.

Hypsicratea fought alongside her husband, and in 67 BCE she helped beat back the armies of a Roman general called Lucullus in an area in central Pontus. Mithradates was severely wounded, but he survived. The following year there was another bloody battle. This time the Roman general Pompey staged a surprise nighttime assault on Mithradates's army. Ten thousand of Mithradates's soldiers were captured. But Mithradates and Hypsicratea slipped away. They galloped off into the almost-vertical snowy mountains and made it all the way to Armenia, where they holed up in one of the king's castles.

At first Pompey thought they'd surely frozen to death in the unforgiving terrain, but he'd underestimated his foes. When Pompey learned they'd survived, he gave chase. The royal couple galloped about five hundred miles farther north. Multiple bands of sympathetic tribes attacked the pursuing Romans, and we can be pretty sure some of them included female Amazon warriors.

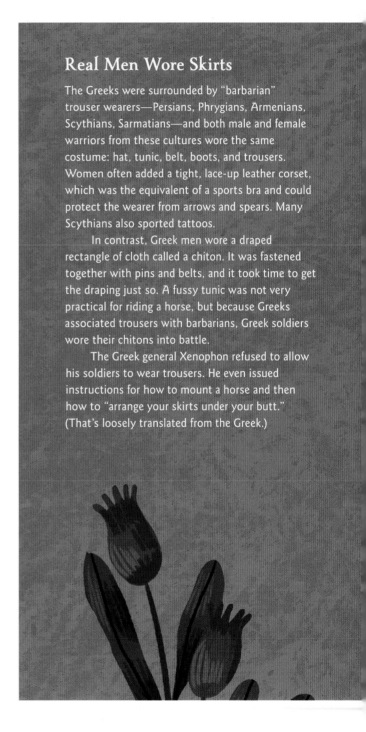

Real Men Wore Skirts

The Greeks were surrounded by "barbarian" trouser wearers—Persians, Phrygians, Armenians, Scythians, Sarmatians—and both male and female warriors from these cultures wore the same costume: hat, tunic, belt, boots, and trousers. Women often added a tight, lace-up leather corset, which was the equivalent of a sports bra and could protect the wearer from arrows and spears. Many Scythians also sported tattoos.

In contrast, Greek men wore a draped rectangle of cloth called a chiton. It was fastened together with pins and belts, and it took time to get the draping just so. A fussy tunic was not very practical for riding a horse, but because Greeks associated trousers with barbarians, Greek soldiers wore their chitons into battle.

The Greek general Xenophon refused to allow his soldiers to wear trousers. He even issued instructions for how to mount a horse and then how to "arrange your skirts under your butt." (That's loosely translated from the Greek.)

Wonder Women

Greek myths were full of magical tales about Amazon warrior women. In ancient Athens, you couldn't throw a brick without cracking an urn or a frieze decorated with images of Amazons.

Here's what ancient Greek writers wrote about the Amazons: They were bands of man-hating warriors. (Nope.) They were all-female societies that mated with strangers once a year. (Wrong.) They killed their male children. (Didn't happen.) They were skilled archers who sometimes poisoned their arrows with snake viper venom. (Okay, that one's probably true.)

Actual Amazons were a loosely connected group of tribes from the Black Sea area, in modern-day Russia. There were both male *and* female members of the tribes. For centuries, they battled with the Greeks.

Archaeologists have dug up burial mounds that reveal warrior women who also had high status in Scythian society. These elite soldiers were buried with bows, swords, jewelry, entire chariots, and horses.

Why did the Greeks make up outrageous tales? Maybe they couldn't fathom the idea that another culture valued women more than the Greeks did. In Athenian families, sons were prized. Daughters were less educated, given less food, and confined to the house till they could be married off. Then they were confined to their husband's house.

So it must have been deeply unsettling to the Greeks to discover a culture where boys and girls dressed alike and where both learned to ride, shoot arrows, defend the tribe, and hunt.

A Greek obsession: Amazons in pants.

Hazy History

By 65 BCE Mithradates had assumed the throne of Pontus once again with Hypsicratea at his side. But then one of his disgruntled sons (from another wife) treacherously betrayed him to the Romans. With General Pompey closing in, Mithradates died by suicide.

After that, Hypsicratea vanishes from the record.

What happened to her? Did she die in battle? Did she take her own life alongside her husband? Was she captured by the Romans? Perhaps she managed to escape back home to Scythia. We have some compelling clues that suggest she survived and lived to a ripe old age.

Here's one possible scenario: According to sources from ancient times, in 47 BCE, sixteen years after Mithradates's death, Roman general Julius Caesar freed a male prisoner of war named Hypsicrates. This prisoner accompanied Caesar on his campaigns and served as a resident historian and an expert on Amazons. Hypsicrates lived to be ninety-two. Could this be our Amazon queen?

Another Tantalizing Trace

In 2010 Russian archaeologists discovered the base of a statue in the waters off the coast of Greece. On it were some chiseled words that honor "Hypsicrates" as the wife of King Mithradates. Sadly the base was all they found. The rest of the statue has been lost. But the date of the inscription is a couple of decades after Mithradates's death, and the place where it was discovered suggests that Hypsicratea stayed alive and well after Mithradates's defeat by the Romans. The statue may have been carved during the reign of one of Mithradates's granddaughters, who had the extremely cool name Queen Dynamis. We may not find out what ultimately happened to Hypsicratea, but then, you never know when a new clue might come to light. For now it's fun to speculate that she survived and thrived.

Khutulun

1260–UNKNOWN

Don't Mess with This Wrestler

In the thirteenth century, nomadic Mongol people traveled on horseback through the high, forbidding terrain of Central Asia. The area was known as the steppes. Children of the steppe region were taught to ride before they could walk. Both boys and girls learned to use bows and arrows. And wrestling was one of the Mongols' favorite pastimes.

It might have looked like fun and games, but the Mongols took their wrestling seriously. Wrestling was a good way to stay physically fit between wars. And who was the undefeated wrestling champ of the thirteenth-century steppe tribes? That would be Princess Khutulun (koo-tuh-LOON). One by one, she threw down all her opponents. No man ever won a match against her.

In Her Honor

Nowadays wrestling is still a hugely popular sport in Mongolia. Male Mongolian wrestlers wear a revealing, open-chested vest for their competitions, which are part of the annual Naadam games—or the Festival of Manly Sports. The uniform design is partly to ensure that a woman can't sneak in to the men-only competition. It would be tough for a woman to disguise herself as a man while wearing a vest with an open chestal area. But the very idea that wrestlers need to prove they're men is a way of acknowledging and honoring the greatest undefeated wrestling champ in history. Who was a woman. Named Khutulun. More than seven hundred years later, Khutulun's undefeated title still stands.

Meet the Family

Khutulun was a great-great-grand-daughter of the powerful Mongol leader Genghis Khan. His well-trained, ruthless soldiers thundered across the steppes on their swift horses and sure-footed donkeys, mowing down standing armies and striking terror throughout the land. By the time he died in his sleep, in 1227, Genghis Khan's empire stretched across most of northern China and westward all the way to eastern Europe. One reason he was so successful was that he promoted his military leaders based on how good they were at their job rather than how important their family was. That was pretty unusual at the time. More shocking still, he sometimes even extended his best-man-for-the-job policy to women.

Kublai Khan, Khutulun's great-uncle.

To cement his power in outlying areas, he sometimes married off his daughters to trustworthy allies. Then he'd install the daughter as queen and demand that her husband come fight in his army.

Khutulun lived in one of these outlying areas. Her father, Kaidu, was the leader of their group. They followed their animal herds around the vast grasslands and mountainous regions of Central Asia, in what's now Mongolia, a country between China and Russia. Khutulun had a lot of brothers. Sources vary, but the number was probably somewhere between fourteen and forty. Presumably she also had a bunch of sisters, although chroniclers seem not to have bothered to count the girls. But Khutulun was her father's favorite. She helped him make decisions about ruling the kingdom. She rode at his side into battle, heading up his army of thousands of warriors. The two of them formed a fearsome fighting team.

Far to the east, in what today is the city of Beijing, was the court of another of Genghis Khan's descendants (and Khutulun's great-uncle), Kublai Khan. He aspired to be the ruler of the entire Mongol Empire. But some of the Mongol states—including that of Khutulun's father—did not approve of Kublai Khan's lavish court and sedentary lifestyle. These groups of tribes lived in what today are Mongolia, Kazakhstan, and the mountainous areas of western China and Kyrgyzstan. Khutulun's group teamed up with others who opposed Kublai Khan's efforts to rule. They remained relatively independent of rule by Kublai Khan's Chinese-style dynasty.

Mongol Ensembles

Besides being a champion wrestler and a Mongol princess, Khutulun was also an excellent horse rider. Like the Scythians before them, the Mongol tribes of the steppes knew that a woman on horseback who possessed a deadly aim with a bow and arrow could be as effective as a man. Although Mongol women didn't typically go to war, they *were* trained in archery. They hunted and defended their homes and flocks while men were away fighting. Mongol women of the steppes enjoyed more freedom than the women in Kublai Khan's court. They did not bind their feet, wear veils, or hide from men.

When Khutulun went to battle at her father's side, she likely wore knee-high leather boots and trousers that buttoned just below the knee. Like most higher-ranking Mongol soldiers, she probably wore a metal helmet and a shirt made of coarse silk. The silk wouldn't tear if an arrow pierced the body, making it easier to yank the arrow out.

For riding, both men and women wore robes that crossed and tied at the waist. The long, wide sleeves extended farther than the fingertips, which allowed the rider to comfortably hold the reins in cold weather.

She Was No Lightweight

As Khutulun grew older, her parents pressured her to marry. So she made a declaration. She would marry the man who could beat her in a wrestling match. In exchange, he'd have to wager some horses for the right to wrestle her. If the

How to Wrestle, the Thirteenth-Century Mongol Way

Stand and face your opponent. At the signal, lunge at him, grab him by the shoulders or the waist, and try to throw him to the ground. Meanwhile your opponent pushes you in the other direction, trying to do the same thing. It's a battle of strength to see who can "throw" the other person, or at least make them touch the ground with something other than their feet. Unlike modern wrestling rules, there are no separate weight categories with the thirteenth-century Mongol mode of wrestling. A low center of gravity helps. Also serious strength and stamina.

suitor lost the match, he'd give Khutulun the horses.

Many men stepped up. She was quite a desirable bride, being a princess and all. But each man who wrestled with her ended up facedown in the turf. She racked up a lot of horses. As in thousands.

Her parents grew concerned. But at long last, at least according to Marco Polo's version, when an especially desirable dude challenged her to wrestle, Khutulun's parents managed to convince her that he was Mr. Right. Even Khutulun conceded that he was "young and handsome, fearless and strong in every way," and he offered a thousand horses as his wager. Khutulun stopped short of agreeing to lose on purpose, but she did promise her parents that she would "gladly be his wife, according to the wager, but not otherwise."

A large crowd gathered to watch. The pair was well matched, and the bout went

Is That a Fact?

Some of what we know about Khutulun comes from an account of the travels of a Venetian explorer named Marco Polo. The writer Rustichello of Pisa published an account of Marco Polo's life around 1300. He based the book on what Marco Polo had told him about his travels to the Far East while the two were imprisoned together in Genoa. Marco Polo had a flair for the dramatic. He described Khutulun as "tall and muscular, so stout and shapely withal, that she was almost like a giantess."

Fortunately we don't have to take Marco Polo's word for it. Other chroniclers have also written about Khutulun, and there's enough overlap of facts that we can be pretty confident that at least the general outline of what we know of her story is true.

A European portrayal of Khutulun (left). She most certainly didn't have blond hair, nor did she wear gowns.

on for some time, with neither opponent able to throw the other. But Khutulun's competitive instincts got the better of her. In front of a live Mongol audience, she heaved her opponent to the ground and won. Oops.

Disgraced and humiliated, the man slunk away. "Great indeed was his shame," a gleeful Marco Polo reported, to have been "thus worsted by a girl!"

Possibly Khutulun regretted having beaten him. Very definitely, her parents were none too pleased. But the upside was that she got to keep the thousand horses.

Chroniclers tell us that eventually she did pick a husband on her own terms. He was "lively, tall, and good-looking." And there's no evidence that he had to wrestle her for her hand in marriage.

But there would be no traditional wifely role for Khutulun. After her marriage she continued to serve in her father's army. According to some accounts, Khutulun's father even gave her a valuable medallion to wear around her neck. Called a *gergee*, it was traditionally worn only by men.

Fade Out

In 1301 Khutulun's father was wounded in battle. He lingered for a month. As he lay dying, he tried to name Khutulun as the next leader of the military. After he died, Khutulun wanted one of her brothers to take her father's place so that she could help with "running affairs." This might suggest that she was interested in helping her brother assume power over the whole group. But there the record dims. We don't know what happened next, except that she died five to fifteen years later. She may have been killed in battle or assassinated.

But her story has lived on in many parts of the world and across centuries. The nineteenth-century Italian composer Puccini wrote an opera about her called *Turandot*.

Nowadays women are still barred from participating in Mongolian wrestling matches, although they do compete in archery and horseback riding. Khutulun was a woman way ahead of her time—and ours.

Joan of Arc

ABOUT 1412–1431

God's Game Plan

Imagine this situation: A seventeen-year-old girl shows up one day at the corporate headquarters of the National Basketball Association. She strides into the office of the NBA commissioner, briefly introduces herself, and then gets straight to the point. She says he must immediately appoint her as the head coach of the worst team in the league, because she and she alone can lead that team to the championships. She has never once touched a basketball and doesn't know the rules of the game.

Partly amused and partly alarmed enough to wonder if he should call security because the girl is clearly unhinged, the commissioner asks her why he should agree to her outlandish request.

Because she's been hearing voices, she patiently explains, and this is what they have told her she needs to do.

Now imagine that her powers of persuasion are so strangely effective that she gets the commissioner to say yes to her daft demands. In a daze, he even hands over his credit card and tells her to go get herself fitted for an expensive new suit, because that's what NBA coaches wear.

Then imagine that she persuades the basketball team—an assortment of large-bodied, short-tempered men—to run her offensive patterns, which are solely based on instinct, not experience. And despite the odds, her team rolls past much better opponents and clinches the championship.

Like *that* would ever happen, right?

Back in the fifteenth century, Joan of Arc, an illiterate peasant girl with zero knowledge of military tactics, pulled off something way more bananas. How did she—a teenage girl—manage to talk high-ranking noblemen into letting her lead outnumbered and demoralized French soldiers into a battle, which they won by beating back an enemy of much-better-trained British invaders? How was she able to persuade the crown prince of France—who had been pushed from power and was holed up in a castle in a faraway part of the kingdom—that she was the one meant to lead him through hostile enemy territory to his coronation ceremony so he could be crowned the rightful king?

The short answer is she must have had great interpersonal skills. She charmed an exhausted and dispirited population of common people because she was a commoner, just like them. Their confidence in her filtered upward through the ranks, all the way to the bedazzled king, who ordered her to be fitted for a new suit of armor polished so brightly it looked white. In Joan's day, such a getup could cost more than an ordinary person's house. The people really believed that God had sent Joan of Arc to save France. And Joan herself was so sure of her own God-fueled mission that anyone who met her became convinced of it too.

Unfortunately, because Joan lived in a century when nearly everyone believed in the existence of magic, witchcraft, and

the devil, her stunned enemies concluded that she could only have accomplished what she did because she was a witch. So her life was short and her death was ghastly, but her legend has lived for six hundred years. And it's still going strong.

Mission: Implausible

We don't know much about what Joan looked like, although judging from some armor believed to have been hers, she was probably about four feet eight inches tall. We know she came from a little village in the northeastern part of France. Like most fifteenth-century French common people, she was extremely religious. Like most people, she believed saints (extremely holy dead people) could work miracles from heaven. Also like most people, she believed that the French king was ordained by God to rule France, and therefore she loathed the English and their aristocratic French allies, known as the Burgundians.

When Joan was twelve, she had a vision. She believed she saw some saints. She believed she heard their voices telling her what to do. As the years passed, her voices grew more urgent. They told her she had been chosen by God to drive out the English invaders, and after that was done, to help the crown prince, called the dauphin, travel through a great swath of enemy-occupied territory to the city of Reims for his coronation.

Joan knew her parents would never let her attempt such a journey. And she knew that as a peasant girl traveling alone, she had no chance of reaching the dauphin. She would need a male to escort her. So she snuck away to a nearby village to find her mother's cousin's husband. She convinced him to help her arrange a meeting with the royal representative in yet another town, a bit farther away. Her goal was to persuade the royal representative to send her to the French royal court of Chinon to see the dauphin. Off they went to arrange the meeting.

This meeting did not go well.

At first the royal representative sent her away, laughing. Nevertheless, she persisted.

Word spread through the town that a young maid had come to rescue France. A few months later, Joan returned for another meeting. By then she'd taken to wearing men's clothes. She'd also cut her hair so short it barely covered her ears. This was a time when women never cut their hair, ever. So Joan's appearance created something of a buzz. (Today in France, this short haircut is still known as "the Joan of Arc.") Then she made a prediction about the outcome of a battle. Several days later, a messenger arrived with news that confirmed the outcome she'd predicted.

Joan in armor.

Now Joan had the royal representative's attention.

He sent word to his boss, a duke named Sir Robert. Sir Robert had already heard about this strange young peasant girl who dressed like a boy and who claimed to be God's chosen messenger. The duke summoned her to a meeting.

By now the citizens of the town were 100 percent behind Joan. They decided that she should be appropriately dressed to meet with a duke, so they swapped out her peasant garb and outfitted her in gentleman's clothing. She showed up at her meeting dressed in a tunic, hose (medieval-style leggings), tight-fitting boots, a cape, and a snug cap atop her cropped hair.

The duke authorized the trip. Joan was given a month-long crash course in how to be a knight. They gave her a sword and a lance. She quickly learned how to use them. They gave her a spirited warhorse. She quickly learned how to ride it.

A crowd gathered to see Joan off. Her band of six escorts included three armed knights and their squires. If these men had been dubious about this harebrained plan at first, Joan soon won them over. Everyone she came into contact with became convinced that this young girl was going to save France.

The 350-mile road trip required passing through hostile territory. After days of grueling and dangerous travel, Joan and her band of fiercely loyal knights arrived at the temporary court of Chinon. Was this peasant girl dressed in men's clothing intimidated by the splendid surroundings? If so, she didn't show it. She went straight to the dauphin, knelt at his feet, and delivered her urgent request: he must agree to let her save his kingdom.

Her powers of persuasion worked. Perhaps the dauphin was as eager for a miracle as everyone else. He commanded someone to fetch her a nicer sword and a nicer horse. He commanded that she be fitted for a fancy suit of armor. Then he sent her off to save France.

Maid of Stern Stuff

The town of Orléans was on the verge of surrendering to the English. Joan rode there with a band of several thousand battle-hardened tough-guy knights, big-name celebrity nobles, and a lot of elite soldiers. She forbade them to fight on holy days, made them go to confession, and told them not to swear. Remarkably they did what she asked.

The two sides clashed—it was the medieval kind of battle where archers rained down arrows from ramparts and people dumped boiling oil from the parapets. Joan herself was shot in the neck with an arrow. She yanked it out, doused the wound with some liniment, and jumped back into the fray. After three days of fighting, the shocked English army retreated. Orléans had been saved.

After the triumph at Orléans, Joan's next task was to get the dauphin to the city of Reims for his formal coronation ceremony. That perilous journey also went off without much of a hitch. She stood by him as he was crowned Charles VII, France's rightful king.

The Backstory: The English and the French Have Never Gotten Along

At the time Joan was born, England and France were in the middle of the Hundred Years' War, an on-again, off-again conflict for control over a chunk of land in what is now northern France. In 1415 English soldiers marched farther into France. There was an epic battle at a place called Agincourt. Using foot soldiers armed with longbows, outnumbered English troops defeated the French, who were still using old-school battle tactics.

By 1420 some of the French nobility (known as Burgundians) decided that England was the winning side. The English and some French Burgundians formed an alliance. They bullied the French heir to the throne, Charles VII (known as the dauphin), into signing a treaty that gave up his right to the crown in favor of an English ruler.

Ordinary French people despised these English invaders and their highborn French conspirators. They believed their king had been chosen by God, and most remained fiercely loyal to the dauphin. But their lives had been made miserable during the long war. Farms and villages had been plundered, and disease and famine had taken a heavy toll.

By the time Joan arrived on the scene, the uncrowned nineteen-year-old Charles VII had fled to a walled city called Chinon to wait out the war. If France won, he'd be king. If England won, he'd lose his throne. And things weren't looking so hot for France. The English armies were on the verge of taking over the rest of the country. English soldiers were besieging the town of Orléans, one of the few remaining cities loyal to Charles VII. If that city fell to the English, most people agreed that the rest of France would too. The French needed a miracle. And they got one—Joan of Arc.

The Battle of Agincourt—foot soldiers and archers for the win.

Joan (shown with long hair) and her English captors.

In just over a year, Joan had grown famous in France and infamous in England. The French common people saw her as the savior of France. The English were convinced she was a witch.

The Bad End

But the long war wasn't over yet. Joan was ambushed and captured by the French Burgundians. They sold their famous prisoner to their English allies. Joan was put in prison and charged with sorcery and witchcraft as well as heresy, which is when someone preaches against the teachings of the church. She stood trial for months, during which she was endlessly questioned by high-ranking, hostile English judges and clergymen. The only upside is that someone wrote down everything she said at her trial. Those records were preserved, and they show that she was honest, incredibly brave, and extremely intelligent. She must have known that telling the judges about the voices bidding her to do God's will would upset church officials. But she was sure she was going to heaven, so she stuck to her story.

Another accusation against Joan—and this was considered almost as unforgivable as being a heretic—was that she'd worn men's clothing. At the time, wearing clothing of the so-called opposite gender was prohibited by divine law. Her interrogators returned again and again to question her about wearing men's clothing. When asked if she thought it was wrong to do so, Joan replied, "No. And even now, if I were with the other side in this clothing of a man, I think it would be one of the best of things for France for me to do as I was doing before my capture!" Joan was doomed.

The French king negotiated for her release and even tried to have her rescued. Nothing worked. Joan was found guilty by the English of witchcraft and heresy and was burned at the stake, which is an especially horrible way to die. She was only about nineteen years old.

The Aftermath

Twenty-two years after Joan's death, Charles VII managed to kick the English out of France once and for all. He ordered an investigation into her trial, and in 1456 she was cleared of heresy charges. Five hundred years after that, the Catholic Church and France recognized her as a saint.

Lady Mary Montagu

1689–1762

A Dismal Disease

Back in the 1700s there were a lot of frightful ways to die young. For example, a small nick from shaving or a prick from a sewing needle could lead to a fatal infection. Childbirth was also fraught with peril. But possibly the illness that people feared most was smallpox. It was a hideous and painful disease, easy to catch and hard to survive. Victims usually suffered from agonizing skin eruptions. If smallpox didn't kill a person, they'd usually be left badly scarred for the rest of their life.

The English writer Mary Wortley Montagu came from an upper-class background, but smallpox did not spare wealthy people any more than it did the poor. Her younger brother died of the disease, leaving behind two young children. When Mary was in her mid-twenties, she too came down with it. She survived, but her face was left permanently scarred. "Poor Lady Mary Wortley has ye small pox," wrote a friend. "She hath them exceedingly full & will be severely markt."

But Lady Mary would soon make her own mark—on history.

Literary Mary

Born Mary Pierrepont in 1689, Mary was the oldest of four children. Her father was an English duke. Her mother, Mary Fielding, died when Mary was a young girl.

When Mary was in her early twenties, her father arranged for her to marry an eligible (code for equally aristocratic) suitor. The man's name was—and this is not a joke—Sir Clotworthy Skeffington. Mary did not want to marry Clotworthy. In 1712 she ran off and married the brother of a friend. His name was Edward Wortley Montagu.

A year later Mary gave birth to a son. By 1715 she had become part of the London literary social scene, hanging around with some of the best-known writers of the day. She was famous for her beauty, but she was more than just a pretty face. Her poems and essays were published and read widely, and she charmed people with her intelligence and wit. One of the people she enchanted was the writer Alexander Pope. Pope was a famous satirist (he wrote witty verse that subtly, and not so subtly, made fun of social injustices), and he seems to have fallen in love with Lady Mary.

Turkish Delight

Shortly after Mary recovered from her bout of smallpox in late 1715, her husband was appointed English ambassador to the Ottoman court. So Mary and Edward and their young son left London. During the two years she lived in Turkey, Mary immersed herself in the culture, particularly the segregated world of women, which was closed to men. She visited the women's baths and the harem and learned to speak Turkish. She enthusiastically took to wearing the Turkish women's style of dress—billowy trousers, veil, and all. With her face veiled, she was able to explore all parts of the city and move freely through the streets without anyone knowing who she was or even that she was a foreigner. In a letter to her sister, she described her trousers with delight. "The first piece of my dress is a pair of drawers, very full, that reach to my shoes and conceal the legs more modestly than your petticoats. They are of a thin, rose-colour damask brocaded with silver flowers."

She had her portrait painted several times wearing her Turkish trousers. She may also have started an art trend. For at least another century, many artists from Western Europe were fascinated by cultures farther to the east, even though most of the artists had never traveled there. They painted inauthentic scenes of what they imagined a Turkish harem might look like, often featuring white women wearing veils and Turkish trousers.

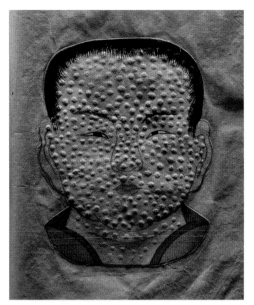

A Japanese medical illustration showing the horrors of smallpox.

Smallpox

Today people no longer get smallpox. But in Lady Mary Montagu's day, this contagious virus killed about one out of every ten people in Europe, and outbreaks occurred every few years. After coming down with flu-like symptoms for a few days, victims broke out in pink spots all over their body. The spots soon developed into painful, pus-filled sores. If a person survived the disease, the sores dried up and eventually fell off but often left the victim severely scarred with pockmarks. Smallpox survivors with pockmarked faces, both young and old, were a regular sight in eighteenth-century towns and cities.

Variolation in Turkey

Lady Mary's Turkish garb was more than just a fashion fad. Her respect for the culture helped her win the trust of people from a different part of the world, and she had enough sense to realize how valuable their knowledge was. She was a rare privileged and educated Westerner who didn't jump to the automatic conclusion that hers was a superior culture. One day while visiting a harem, Lady Mary witnessed a procedure called engraftment variolation. She wrote to her friend about what she had seen. "The smallpox, so fatal and so general amongst us, is here entirely harmless by the invention of engrafting (which is the term they give it)." She wondered how many lives could be saved back in her own country.

Warning: if you are easily grossed out, skip the next sentence.

The procedure involved taking fresh pus from an oozing sore of a smallpox victim and scratching it into the skin of a healthy person (or drying it out and blowing it up their nostrils).

Variolation had been practiced for centuries in parts of Africa, the Middle East, and Asia. Smallpox variolation was known to a few English physicians, but the procedure was viewed with suspicion. So it was rarely performed in England.

Alexander Pope declares his love for Lady Mary while she laughs.

For one thing, the procedure was risky. A small percentage of healthy people contracted the full-blown disease and died. Another problem was that the variolated people remained contagious for several weeks, thus endangering others. Still, Mary became convinced that variolation was way better than doing nothing.

While still in Turkey, Lady Mary resolved to try the process on her own five-year-old son. Only a few months earlier, she'd given birth to a daughter, but she didn't dare have the procedure done on her baby, because the child's nurse had never had smallpox and might have become infected.

In the same letter, Mary continued, "You may believe I am very well satisfied of the safety of the experiment since I intend to try it on my dear little son. I am patriot enough to take pains to bring this useful invention into fashion in England."

Mary instructed the embassy doctor Charles Maitland to oversee her son as he was variolated, or inoculated, in the Turkish manner. The procedure was performed by an old Turkish woman known for her skill with the procedure. Mary's son recovered and, as did all smallpox survivors, he became immune to the disease. A few months later, the family sailed back to England.

Getting the Word Out

Remember Alexander Pope? By this time, Mary was no longer friends with him. In fact, for unknown reasons, they'd had a very public disagreement and had become bitter enemies. It's unclear what the quarrel was about. One theory is that when Pope, an odd-looking man who stood only about four foot six, declared his love to her, she laughed out loud. So his new favorite hobby was to write mean things about her in practically every essay he published.

As soon as she was back in England, Mary tried to spread the word about the remarkable technique she'd learned of in Turkey. Unfortunately Mary couldn't get people on board. For one thing she was a woman, and a woman's know-how wasn't respected. For another, her ex-friend Alexander Pope was busy writing a lot of spiteful poems about her, and everyone read his work.

Then another smallpox outbreak struck London. Mary decided to have her now-four-year-old daughter undergo variolation. It would be a win-win: not only would Mary be able to protect her child, but she could also publicly prove her point. The procedure was performed by Mary's nervous physician, who insisted on several other attendants as witnesses. The child became mildly ill

The Cure at Last

Sixteen years after Mary Montagu's death (she lived to be ninety-two), a country doctor named Edward Jenner made a discovery. He observed that milkmaids who had contracted cowpox, an illness similar to smallpox but much less serious, seemed immune to smallpox. He experimented with inoculating people with cowpox particles taken from the hand of a milkmaid. He found that people developed a mild case of cowpox but were left immune to smallpox. In 1798 he published his findings. In his paper, he used the term "vaccination" to describe the procedure—from *vaca*, the Latin word for cow. His vaccination using cowpox proved considerably safer than the variolation procedure, which used actual smallpox. By 1800 his vaccination was introduced throughout Europe and the Americas, and the procedure later spread to other parts of the world. It was considered by many to be the greatest medical achievement of the age.

Kids have never liked needles, but vaccinations save lives.

and recovered. The method so impressed one of the men who witnessed it—he had lost a son to smallpox—that he immediately had his surviving child variolated.

The antivirus news went viral, eighteenth-century style.

Many of Mary's friends had their own children variolated. Even Caroline, the princess of Wales, who was a friend of Mary's, grew intrigued. The princess decided to experiment on six condemned criminals. They agreed to the procedure. If they survived, they would be granted a royal pardon and set free. The procedure was performed in front of many witnesses. All the prisoners survived. Still not convinced, the princess ordered all the orphans in an orphanage to undergo the treatment. (Yep. You read that right. And to think this period is known as the Age of Enlightenment.) The orphans all survived. Finally she agreed to variolate her three daughters.

Many members of the clergy railed against the procedure, claiming that it interfered with the will of God. Some physicians were also unconvinced, not wanting to trust "an Experiment practiced only by a few *Ignorant Women*, amongst an illiterate and unthinking People." The "ignorant women" jab, which Mary probably took personally, caused her to take up her pen and write a furious response.

Her essay was printed in a popular London paper. But she didn't use her real name. She wrote as an anonymous author and claimed she was a merchant who had done business in Turkey. The essay was called "A Plain Account of ye Inoculating of ye Small Pox." Of *course* everyone assumed the "merchant" was a man.

In the first paragraph, Mary wrote, "I am determined to give a true account of the manner of inoculating the small pox as it is practiced at Constantinople with constant success, and without any ill consequence whatever." The essay sparked debate and controversy among physicians and clergymen.

The Power of Her Pen

Mary's 1721 essay was published sixty years before a safer smallpox vaccination was discovered. She was a woman who spoke her mind—her brilliant mind— and she was way ahead of her time. She didn't profit from her crusade since she didn't use her real name in her published appeal to adopt the procedure. As she put it, "I shall get nothing by it but the private satisfaction of having done good to mankind." After that essay was published, the rate of inoculation through variolation rose. It had worked.

For two hundred years, until Mary's private papers were made public, no one knew the real identity of the unnamed person who had published that impassioned argument in favor of variolation.

But now *you* know her name.

Anne Bonny

ABOUT 1698–ABOUT 1782

Mary Read

ABOUT 1690–1721

Foul-Weather Friends

When you think of a pirate, what picture pops into your mind? You might conjure up an image of a scruffy man with a patch on his eye, a parrot on his shoulder, and dubious personal hygiene. But did you know there were female pirates too? There were female Viking pirates and female China Sea pirates, and even female pirates of the Caribbean.

Two of these female pirates were named Anne Bonny and Mary Read. They sailed in the early part of the 1700s, along the North American coast, around the Caribbean, and as far away as the Indian Ocean. And both women were as fierce and feisty as any brazen buccaneer who sailed the seven seas.

Motley Mates

Anne Bonny and Mary Read were pirate shipmates for a brief time. Although they came from different backgrounds, both women became pirates because they had nothing to lose. Pirating was dangerous, sure, but it offered freedom to escape from a life of drudgery, a chance to earn decent money, and a rare opportunity to see the world. Not a terrible trade-off, when you think about it.

Here are the general outlines of each one's journey to a life of crime aboard the same pirate ship.

Anne's Tale

Anne was born in Ireland in about 1698. Her father, William Cormac, was an attorney. But Anne's mother was not William Cormac's wife. While his wife was pregnant with twins and living with William's mother, William got the servant-maid pregnant with Anne. Awkward.

Anne's mother gave birth to her about the same time that William Cormac's wife gave birth to the twins. Anne's father tried to conceal the fact that he had this daughter. He had Anne "put into Breeches, as a Boy, pretending it was a Relation's Child he was to breed up to be his Clerk," according to one chronicler. His wife didn't buy it. She went public with her husband's affair, and got her in-laws to cut him off from his inheritance.

So William, Anne's mother, and baby Anne fled the country. They moved to Charles Town (now known as Charleston, South Carolina). William managed to make a new fortune and bought a plantation.

Anne's mother died when Anne was about twelve, and over the next several years Anne helped run the plantation. She was known for her fiery temper. Eventually her father picked out a guy

for Anne to marry, but she refused. Instead she married a common sailor named James Bonny. Anne's biographer described him as "a young Fellow, who belonged to the Sea, and was not worth a Groat." (A groat was a coin worth just a few cents.)

Big mistake. Anne's father disowned her. She now had no money, which was problematic, because her husband appears to have wanted to marry her only *for* her money. She soon dumped her husband and escaped to sea "in Men's Cloaths" with her new boyfriend, a guy named John Rackham. John also happened to be a pirate captain who went by the picturesque name of Calico Jack.

Early on, Anne seems to have passed as a seaman among the pirate crew. Like her shipmates, she dressed in a tunic and loose-fitting trousers made of canvas sailcloth. But soon enough she dropped the ruse and pirated openly as a woman, though still dressed in men's clothing.

Then one day a young sailor named Mark Read joined up with the crew. To Calico Jack's dismay, Anne developed a crush on the handsome blond sailor. Then Anne discovered that the handsome blond sailor was another woman in disguise. Her name was Mary Read. As one eighteenth-century writer recounted, Calico Jack got so jealous that

Grime and Punishment

A young man in the eighteenth century with a hankering for a life at sea had a couple of options. He could join the navy and become a lawful sailor. Or he could become a pirate.

For a woman, going to sea held a certain appeal if she fell on hard times and wanted to avoid a life of begging or prostitution. But her options were considerably more complicated. Because women were barred from the navy, the only way for a woman to join up was to disguise herself as a man.

While *all* eighteenth-century ships were reeking, crowded, and disease-ridden, life on a navy ship was especially un-fun. The captain ruled. Punishments for breaking rules could be harsh. Ordinary sailors toiled day after day at boring, physically demanding tasks alongside shipmates who hadn't bathed in weeks. The food was terrible (and scanty). And a woman in disguise always faced the danger of being discovered and punished.

So the second option for nautically inclined women, pirating, had a strong appeal.

Life on a pirate ship was dismal too, but a notch better than on navy ships. For one, the rules were less strict. Captains were elected at the start of every voyage. Everyone voted when it came to deciding when to raid or where to sail next. Plus everyone got a share of the booty. A pirate ship could also be a multicultural marvel, with crews hailing from all over the world. If you were good at pirating, no one cared about the color of your skin or your family background. Or even about your gender, in certain cases.

But pirating was dangerous. Besides the usual perils, pirates faced the ever-present risk of being killed, captured, or executed.

Anne and Mary in their pirate attire.

he threatened to "cut her new Lover's Throat." And "therefore, to quiet him, [Anne] let him into the Secret also."

Mary's Tale

How did Mary Read end up a pirate? Her mother was married to an English sailor. He went off to sea when Mary's mother was pregnant with their child. Then the husband disappeared. Mary's biographer explains, "Whether he was cast away, or died in his Voyage, Mary Read could not tell; but however, he never returned more." Mary's mother gave birth to the child, a boy, and moved in with her absent husband's family. Then she became pregnant again—with Mary—inconvenient, given that her husband was lost at sea and couldn't possibly be the father. It was doubly problematic because she was living with her absent husband's family. Mary's mother quickly left her in-laws' home and moved in with friends. Her first child, Mary's half brother, died shortly before Mary was born, in 1690. Because her mother-in-law was still sending money to support the boy, Mary's mother had to do some quick thinking. She dressed baby Mary in boys' clothing to trick the mother-in-law into believing the boy had lived. That worked.

Mary was dressed as a boy for the first thirteen years of her life. Then her step-grandma died and the money dried up. Mary's mother "was obliged to put her Daughter out, to wait on a French Lady, as a Foot-boy." That was a boy who ran in front of his boss's carriage and watched out for potholes and tree stumps. He also ran ahead to make hotel and dinner reservations. This job did not suit Mary. When she was about fifteen, she landed a position as a crew member in the royal navy. She wasn't crazy about that job either. Probably realizing how few options she had as a woman, she kept wearing her male disguise and went off job-searching.

She traveled to Flanders (now part of Belgium) and joined the English army. But then the war ended and once again she needed a way to support herself. So she hopped "a Vessel bound for the West-Indies."

Here the story gets hazy again. Some accounts say her ship was captured by Calico Jack's pirate ship, and she was forced to join up with them. Others say she willingly joined the pirate crew—in the guise of a handsome blond sailor, Mark Read. However it happened, she and Anne Bonny became friends. They proved to be excellent pirates, as willing to fight and curse and drink and rob as any of their male comrades.

The Capture

Officials of the British Empire had grown tired of having its merchant ships attacked and plundered all over the world. The English navy began a campaign to crack down on pirates. One day navy pirate-hunters attacked Calico Jack's ship somewhere near Jamaica. With the rest of the crew belowdecks snoring off a groggy binge, Anne and Mary tried to fend off the attackers all by themselves. But they were outnumbered. Anne, Mary, Calico Jack, and the rest of the crew were captured.

The Trial

They were put on trial in 1720, accused of "Piracies, Felonies, and Robberies . . . on the High Sea." Witnesses and former victims testified that the two women "wore Men's Jackets, and long Trouzers, and Handkerchiefs tied about their Heads: and that each of them had a Machet and Pistol in their Hands and cursed and Swore at the Men."

Some of the women's shipmates were released because they claimed to have been press-ganged, or forced, into piracy. The remaining pirates were sentenced to hang, including Calico Jack, Mary, and Anne.

It was at that point that both women claimed to be pregnant. This defense was called "pleading the belly." Because the court didn't want to take an innocent life along with a guilty one, their executions were postponed until after their babies were born. It's unclear if either was really pregnant.

The day before his execution, Calico Jack asked to see his beloved Anne one last time. According to lore, the fiery-tempered Anne flounced to his cell and regarded him disdainfully. Her last words to him? She was sorry to see him there, but "If he had fought like a Man, he need not have been hang'd like a Dog." Ouch.

The Tale Trails Off

Court records show that neither Anne nor Mary was executed, but we don't know for sure what happened to them. Mary seems to have died of a fever—or perhaps during childbirth—while still in prison. Anne was released for reasons unknown. Maybe her rich father heard from his influential friends that his daughter was in prison and bailed her out. Maybe she escaped and joined up with a new crew in a new disguise. Whatever their fate, Anne and Mary's lives have remained a source of fascination ever since.

Deborah Sampson

1760–1827

Reporting for Duty

The last major battle of the American Revolutionary War was at Yorktown, Virginia, in October 1781. The British general Lord Cornwallis surrendered to General George Washington. With help from France, the Americans had won the war. But news traveled slowly back then, and peace treaties took a long time to hammer out. Even after Yorktown, the British army still occupied New York City, and skirmishes continued throughout the colonies. No one quite knew when the war would be truly over, and the Continental (American) Army continued to sign up new soldiers.

So in the spring of 1782, recruiters in central Massachusetts were pleased when a tall, clean-shaven young man named Robert Shurtliff reported for duty.

Little did they know that Robert Shurtliff was a woman in disguise.

A Self-Made Man

Robert Shurtliff's real name was Deborah Sampson (sometimes spelled Samson). She seems to have fooled basically everyone. A few women before her had tried to join the American army disguised as men. They'd been caught, severely disciplined, and then drummed out of camp. But Deborah got away with it because she had some things working in her favor.

First, uniforms at the time were cut in such a way that they could make soldiers of all shapes and sizes look more or less, well, uniform. Beneath her roomy jacket, Deborah wrapped linen cloth tightly around her chest to flatten it. She was also tall for an eighteenth-century woman—about five foot seven—and she was as strong as the average man. Her higher voice and lack of facial stubble fit right in with the as-yet-unchanged voices and smooth faces of the many teenage boys who enlisted.

Poor Girl

Deborah was born into a large family, the fifth of seven kids. Her father, a farm laborer, abandoned the family when Deborah was about five. Unable to feed everyone, Deborah's mother was forced to farm out the kids to other households, where they worked as indentured servants. Deborah eventually ended up living with a large family named the Thomases. For eight years, in exchange for a room and meals, she served them. During that time, she picked up a lot of skills. She taught herself to read. She learned how to weave, spin, and sew. She learned how to take care of kids. And she performed a lot of heavy farm chores, including plowing. She grew strong and lean.

On her eighteenth birthday, she was released from servitude. The year was 1778. The American Revolution was in full swing.

Deborah had reached a perilous point in her life. As a young, single woman without money, a home, or protection, she didn't have many options for earning a living. For a while she managed to support herself as a thread spinner and cloth weaver, and she lived at various neighbors' homes in Middleborough, Massachusetts. She found the work tedious and boring.

So here's what may have been her line of thinking: She could choose option one and get married. This was by no means a sure thing. First off, even if there were an eligible bachelor around—this was wartime, so all the young men were off fighting—Deborah had no money or land or family name, which were things that mattered a lot to potential marriage partners in the eighteenth century. And second off, at the Thomas farm, she had seen firsthand what was in store for her if she married a local farmer—a life of hard work and lots of kids.

Which left her with option two: disguise herself as a man and join the army.

There *was* no option three by Deborah's reckoning. She was young and smart. She wanted to see the world. She

Deborah in a dress, painted after her soldier days.

through various towns toward the coast and then zigzagging north to Boston. Perhaps she thought about becoming a sailor and changed her mind. From Boston, she headed southwest until she got to the Massachusetts town of Bellingham. There she enlisted in the Continental Army.

A Suitable Soldier

It turned out to be relatively easy to convince the recruiting officers that she was male. They were so eager for new recruits, they didn't ask too many questions, and they most likely didn't perform a physical exam. They handed her a uniform and a signing bonus and packed her off to join Washington's army in New York.

Upon arriving at the base near West Point, north of New York City, she was assigned to an elite unit known as the Light Infantry.

Soldiers chosen for the Light Corps, as it was also called, were tall, young, athletic, and intelligent. They were light on equipment so they could go on scouting missions that required endurance and mobility. They were the best of the best, kind of like the eighteenth-century version of today's Navy SEALs. As one historian notes, "Officers in search of glory, like Alexander Hamilton, begged for assignment to the light infantry."

wanted experiences. She made herself a suit of clothes and purchased men's shoes and a hat. She bound her chest, put on her new outfit, and set off on foot for the nearest army recruiting station. She decided her name would be Robert Shurtliff.

Her first effort was in her own small town, but that didn't work out. Everyone knew her, and her disguise was quickly discovered. So she resolved to travel farther away, to a place where no one knew her. With no money for a coach, she'd have to walk.

Deborah-as-Robert trudged more than 150 miles, wending her way south

How Did She Go to the Bathroom?

Soldiers' breeches had a "front fall," which was a flap that buttoned across the waist. A male soldier unfastened the buttons and let the flap flop down so he could pee standing up. Deborah would have had to pull down her breeches and squat. So she probably did a lot of stealing away into the woods. Or maybe she tried to go only after dark. Even male soldiers had to lower their breeches to go number two, so maybe her comrades just assumed that's what she was doing if they spotted her squatting.

She served for the next seventeen months and wasn't found out, even while living in close quarters with her fellow soldiers. She stood out as a superior soldier among an already-elite group of soldiers. She was so good at acting like a man, no one ever stopped to consider that she hadn't been born one. It also helped that soldiers slept in their clothes.

Discovered

The war was mostly over by June 1783, but skirmishes were still frequent. Deborah and two sergeants led about thirty other infantrymen on an expedition and clashed with a band of enemy soldiers. During the encounter, Deborah was slightly wounded by a sword gash to the head and more seriously by a musket ball, probably to the upper thigh. According to one source, she was able to conceal the second wound from the doctors and extracted the musket ball herself using rum to clean the wound and digging it out with a knife and a sewing needle. Hard-core.

Later that summer, with the war finally drawing to a close, Deborah's unit was ordered to march from West Point to Philadelphia. Some sort of epidemic was raging in Philadelphia. Soon after arriving, Deborah came down with a fever—it may have been measles, which could be deadly. Deborah was sent to the military hospital.

Soldiers and civilians were dying right and left. Deborah, her fever raging, slipped into unconsciousness. A doctor who was attempting to determine if she was alive and breathing unwound the linen bandages binding her chest. He discovered her secret. He informed General John Paterson. Perhaps because of her exemplary service, or perhaps because everyone was in a good mood for having won the war, General Paterson allowed her to remain in uniform. After she recovered, Deborah was honorably discharged at West Point in October 1783 along with the rest of her unit.

The Story Goes Public

Three months later, the *New York Gazette* sniffed out the story. The article noted that "a lively comely young nymph, 19 years old, dressed in man's apparel has been discovered; and what redounds [contributes] to her honor, she has served in the character of a soldier for near three years undiscovered." She was actually closer to twenty-three when she was discharged, and it was a stretch to say she'd served three years, but whatever. It made for a good read.

By then, Deborah had already walked all the way to Sharon, Massachusetts, still in men's clothing, where she stayed with an aunt. At that point she switched back to women's clothing, and about a year after that, she got married.

Her husband's name was Benjamin Gannett Jr., and he doesn't seem to have possessed Deborah's ambition or gusto. Deborah gave birth to their first child, a boy named Earl. Deborah and Benjamin struggled to make ends meet on their small farm. After two more kids came along, Deborah resolved to improve the family's financial status herself.

She petitioned the state of Massachusetts for her soldier's pension, including back pay. She believed in giving credit where credit was due, and she was due. Incredibly, the legislature agreed— the order was signed by Governor John Hancock. Yes, that John Hancock.

In 1802 she went on the lecture circuit. She delivered at least twenty lectures around New York and New England, talking to paying audiences about her experiences as a soldier. Sometimes she put on her soldier's uniform, and she entertained her audience by doing cool tricks handling her musket. She continued to petition Congress for more of her pension. General Paterson, the same general who had permitted her honorable discharge, supported her petition. Even Paul Revere—yes, that Paul Revere— helped write letters on her behalf. Finally, in 1805, she was granted four dollars per month by the US government (which was decent pay back then).

Few women in Deborah's day fought in wars or argued with Congress or went on lecture circuits. Deborah did all those things. Eventually, she and her husband inherited his father's larger farmhouse, and they lived there until she died in 1827, at the age of sixty-seven.

THREE-THOUSAND-AND-SOMETHING DAYS

Jeanne Baret

1740–1807

What a Guy

In 1766 the king of France announced his plan to send an expedition on a voyage around the world. The purpose was to explore new lands, meet new people, and study new plants and animals, all for the glory of France. Ships from Britain, the Netherlands, and Spain had already sailed around the world, and the French king didn't want to be left behind.

The captain of the expedition, Louis-Antoine de Bougainville, invited a well-respected scientist to come along on the three-year voyage. The scientist's name was Philibert de Commerson. His job was to look for and collect plants, animals, and insects that were new to the French.

As Commerson prepared to board the ship, a young man approached and introduced himself. The young man said his name was Jean (a French name sort of like "John" in English). Jean asked Philibert de Commerson if he needed an assistant for the voyage. Commerson hired the young man on the spot.

But there was something odd about Commerson's new assistant. His name wasn't actually Jean. In fact he was not a "he" at all. "He" was a woman in disguise. Her real name was Jeanne Baret, and Philibert de Commerson knew her well.

In fact, she was his girlfriend. They'd been living together for years. After Commerson's wife died, he'd hired Jeanne as his housekeeper and assistant. She was a skilled herbalist—someone who knew how to recognize and collect plants. They fell in love. But because he was a member of the upper class, and she was from a peasant background, it wasn't proper for them to marry.

In eighteenth-century France, an herbalist like Jeanne who had knowledge of medicinal plants was often the only medical helper most peasants ever saw. Herbalists, sometimes known as wise women, learned their craft not from books but by passing knowledge orally from one generation to the next. They collected plants and delivered them to apothecaries (eighteenth-century-style pharmacists) and physicians. Most university-trained physicians—all males, of course—looked down their noses at these mostly illiterate women, even though the physicians had no idea where to find or identify medicinal plants in the wild.

Commerson recognized that Jeanne was a talented plant expert, even if she probably couldn't read and write. He was also not in great health. He knew he would need Jeanne's help during the voyage. Because French navy ships had a "no women allowed" policy, he and Jeanne hatched a plan for her to disguise herself as a young man. If Jeanne posed as a nobleman's manservant, her inexperience with ships and sailing wouldn't seem suspicious.

Jeanne's disguise probably resembled the clothing of a common French sailor—she likely wore a baggy linen smock over wide, puffy trousers, a kerchief around her neck, and no shoes.

The First Phase of the Voyage

There were two ships on the expedition, and for the first part of the voyage, Commerson and Jeanne sailed on the smaller supply ship. Being landlubbers, they were both horribly seasick as their creaky, leaky ship crossed the Atlantic. The ship lurched over huge swells and shuddered through teeth-rattling gales. To explain to the others on the ship why "Jean" had to share a cabin with Commerson, they made up a story about how Jean had to take care of the collected samples and look after the ailing Commerson. Still, it was extremely unusual for a gentleman to share a cabin with a servant. Servants always slept with the common sailors. The other sailors on board probably grew suspicious of the pair right away.

Also, Jeanne never went to the bathroom in front of anyone. Regular sailors relieved themselves at the head, which was a hole cut out of the forward deck of the ship, visible to everyone. There were about 115 men living on the ship. Imagine how hard it must have been for Jeanne to maintain her disguise around

all those people smooshed together in cramped quarters.

They crossed the Atlantic and joined up with the main ship on the coast of South America. There, Jeanne and Commerson met Captain Bougainville, who had sailed on the other vessel. If the captain suspected that Jeanne was a woman or that she and the chief scientist were a couple, he kept it to himself. If the French navy found out he'd allowed a woman to travel this far, he might damage his own reputation.

The first official stop was Rio de Janeiro, Brazil. Jeanne and Commerson left the ship nearly every day to go collecting. She probably carried most of the gear, which included a spade, glass vials for seeds, tiny boxes for insects, magnifying glasses, a telescope, a compass, wooden presses, and a butterfly net.

One day when Commerson was too ill to leave the ship, Jeanne went off by herself to gather specimens. She returned with a beautiful vine. Commerson named it after Captain Bougainville. Today you can find the flowering plant called bougainvillea in lots of gardens all around the world, including the United States.

Life at Sea

The two ships continued their voyage, sailing around the tip of South America and into the vast Pacific Ocean. It must have been a thrill for Jeanne to see penguins, sea lions, and whales. She had never before traveled more than twenty miles from her small French village, yet now she hiked through tropical forests and gazed up at huge, icy glaciers. During one part of the voyage they crossed the equator. Not long after that, four inches of snow fell on the deck.

There were also difficult times, when food ran low and the crew was forced to drink stinky water and eat roasted rats for dinner.

Bougainvillea, which Jeanne introduced to Europeans.

The only image that exists of Jeanne, painted several decades after her death.

Dumped

It's not entirely clear when Jeanne's secret was found out. It may have occurred when they landed on the island of Tahiti in the middle of the Pacific Ocean. Some accounts say that the people native to the island knew right away that she was a woman and helpfully pointed it out. Others say that her fellow sailors waited for the chance to confront her and tore off her clothes, showing that Jean was really Jeanne.

However it really came about, Captain Bougainville had no choice but to get Jeanne off his ship, because women weren't allowed on French navy ships. He deposited Jeanne and Commerson at a place called Île de France (modern-day Mauritius), a French-colonized island in the Indian Ocean, off the east coast of Africa. Then, with a cordial farewell, he and the expedition continued back to France.

Here's where yet another colorful character enters the story. The governor of the French colony was a one-armed former pirate named Pierre Poivre. He was also an enthusiastic plant collector, and he welcomed Commerson into his home. Jeanne, now openly a woman, was given a room too—in the servants' quarters.

The Return

Philibert de Commerson's health grew worse and worse. After about a year on the island, he died at the age of forty-five. (Jeanne was thirty-two.) His specimens—many of them collected by Jeanne—were shipped back to France.

What now? Jeanne was no longer under Commerson's protection. She was a single woman with no way to support herself, all alone on an island in the Indian Ocean with no ride home. She somehow landed on her feet. She found work as an herbalist and barmaid. After seven years on the island, she met and married a French sailor. They sailed back to France.

That made her the first woman ever to circumnavigate—sail all the way around—the world. There was no crowd to cheer for her at the docks in France, but what she'd done was remarkable. And happily, Jeanne learned that Commerson had left her a small sum of money in his will. It was enough for her and her husband to start a new life in the village where he had grown up.

About ten years later, the French government acknowledged Jeanne as the first woman to sail all the way around the world, and she was given a pension for life. Perhaps Captain Bougainville helped to arrange it. He had become a celebrity by that time, and his written account of the voyage was a best seller. Jeanne and her husband lived happily ever after, and she died at the relatively advanced age of sixty-seven.

Jeanne left no record (probably because she didn't know how to write), so we may never know all the details of her remarkable journey. We have only others' accounts to go by. But she was clearly an adventurous, brave person who endured hardships and dangers and did what she loved. At a time in history when poor and uneducated women had few options to explore, travel, and pursue scientific passions, this woman managed to do all three.

Running Eagle

ABOUT 1810–ABOUT 1850

Rider and Raider

Running Eagle was called by many names during her lifetime, and one of them was chief. Addressing a woman by such an honored title was unusual among the Native people who lived on the Great Plains of North America— including the Blackfoot, Running Eagle's tribe. Roles for men and women were strictly defined. Men were the warriors, hunters, and shamans (spiritual leaders). Nineteenth-century artists—both Native and European—loved to paint pictures of male warriors.

Meanwhile, painters weren't exactly clamoring to render Native women as they went about performing their traditional roles. Blackfoot women were too busy—tending vegetables, preparing meals, scraping guts from animal skins to turn them into hides (a process known as tanning), making clothing, collecting firewood, lugging water, setting up camp, and birthing and taking care of kids—to thunder across the plains on the back of a glossy steed.

But Running Eagle was no ordinary girl. So what did Running Eagle do to earn the title of chief and to achieve fame in song and story? As is often the challenge with nomadic cultures, which pass stories orally rather than in written form, it can be difficult to separate the facts of Running Eagle's life from the legend she later became. But here is the gist of what historians think they know about her.

A Blackfoot chief who lived about the same time as Running Eagle.

Her Tribe

Running Eagle's parents gave her the name Otaki at birth, which loosely translates into English as "Brown Weasel Woman." Otaki came from a group of people who were part of the Blackfoot Nation. The Blackfoot moved around a vast area in the middle of the continent on the land that today makes up northern Montana; Idaho; and Alberta, Canada.

There were four loosely connected divisions of Blackfoot people who shared a similar language and culture and were governed by a council of chiefs from each division. The three Canadian divisions were called the Pikani, the Kainai, and the Siksika. The American group was called the Blackfeet. Otaki's group was the Pikani, which translates into English roughly as "people with black feet." This is probably a reference to their black-soled moccasins, or perhaps it's related to the charred black soil they walked on as they moved around the prairie, following buffalo. Life on the Great Plains for Otaki and her people involved frequent violent clashes between the Blackfoot and many other neighboring tribes. Relations between the Blackfoot and white settlers were tense, since treaties between the US government and the Blackfoot were often broken by the government.

Her Early Years

Otaki was the oldest of four or five siblings. Here's a rough outline of what we think we know about her: As a kid she seemed to prefer dressing in boys' clothing. That meant her outfit would likely have been a shirt or buckskin tunic and a belted breechcloth, which is a long cloth that winds over the belt, between the legs, and then over the belt in the back. In cold weather she probably pulled on leggings made of animal skins and would have worn moccasins too. Blackfoot girls and women mostly wore dresses made of deerskin. Fancier tunics and dresses were fringed and decorated with porcupine quills, beads, and animal teeth. In winter everyone wore buffalo-hide robes.

Harrowing Hunting

As a young girl Otaki begged her father to teach her skills traditionally taught only to boys, such as how to shoot a bow and arrow, hunt, and ride a horse. Her father taught her these skills, and she took to them quickly. Eventually, and against her mother's wishes, Otaki was allowed to join men on buffalo-hunting expeditions. Otaki's tribe depended on buffalo for food, clothing, and supplies. The massive animals roamed the plains in huge herds. Imagine how much courage it took to face a two-ton, angry animal roughly eleven feet long and six feet tall. But Otaki was the type who thought that facing a charging buffalo was more fun than staying home doing housework.

One day while hunting, Otaki's group encountered a surprise attack by an enemy tribe. As her group turned and fled, Otaki's father's horse was shot out from under him. The rest of the men galloped away. Otaki turned her horse, thundered back into the fray, hauled her father up and onto her own horse, and escaped with him.

Who *Were* All These Enemy Warriors?

Life on the Great Plains was not very peaceful in the nineteenth century. As more and more Native people were forced to move westward to escape disease and the takeover of their lands by white settlers, tribal warfare flared. The Blackfoot were enemies of the Crow, the Sioux, and the Salish.

Two Spirit

In many Native cultures across North America, people have long believed that there are more than just two genders (boy/man and girl/woman). It has been accepted that some people wear the dress and perform tribal duties of a gender other than the one they were assigned at birth, and many communities have specific terms in their own language for these community members. More recently the term "two spirit" has been introduced in English for this phenomenon across many Indigenous cultures.

When nineteenth-century Europeans encountered gender-fluid members of Native American communities, many were shocked and disapproving.

And when white people imposed their values on Native cultures, forcing tribes off their land and onto reservations, and enrolling Native children in schools where their tribal heritage and languages were erased, they sought to crush the practice of gender fluidity as well. Boarding-school teachers, missionaries, and government agents punished and shamed people into dressing and behaving according to white people's expectations.

In many Native communities today people continue to embrace and honor the two spirit role and its traditions.

while enemy warriors are shooting arrows at you. Back at camp, Otaki was honored for her courageous deed, and for a long time after, the story about her bravery was told around many a campfire.

When Otaki was about fifteen, her mother became seriously ill. As the oldest child, it fell upon Otaki to care for her mother and take over the cooking and tanning and housework and babysitting. She performed her duties, but she probably did a lot of muttering "I'd rather be buffalo hunting."

Then her father was killed by enemy warriors. Soon after Otaki's family learned that news, Otaki's sickly mother died too. Suddenly finding herself and her siblings orphans, Otaki took charge. She invited a recently widowed woman to move in with them to care for the younger kids and do the household chores. Then Otaki donned warrior wear, shouldered her dead father's weapons, and rejoined the men.

Warrior Woman

When Otaki was about twenty, she joined a raiding party to reclaim some horses that had been stolen by some Crow warriors. She crept into their camp and made off with six horses (some accounts say eleven). When the Crow warriors realized what happened, they pursued Otaki and

That showed warrior-grade strength and courage. Pulling a grown man from the ground up onto a horse at full gallop requires immense upper-body strength and agility, no matter how good the man's vertical leap might be. Let alone the others over the course of several days. One night when Otaki was keeping watch, two enemy warriors entered the camp. She singlehandedly fought them off, saving the herd of horses.

Her fellow warriors overcame their reluctance at the idea of fighting alongside a female warrior. Some believed she was endowed with supernatural powers. At the suggestion of some elders, Otaki went on a vision quest: a rite of passage where a young person goes alone to a solitary place for four days and four nights, eating nothing and waiting for a visitation from a spirit to show them their destiny. When Otaki returned, she reported that she'd had a spiritual vision of the sun.

She was invited to participate in a Sun Ceremony at the medicine lodge. That was usually an exclusively male ceremony, and that's where the tribe's chief bestowed a new name upon her—Running Eagle, or P'tamaka. It was an ancient name and a big honor. She was invited into the Braves Society, which was kind of like getting picked for the all-star team.

Running Eagle proved to be super-skilled at leading raids, and more and more warriors wanted to join her party. Her warrior uniform probably consisted of leggings, a shirt, and a breechcloth. She probably carried a rawhide war shield.

For some time—possibly many years—she continued to lead war parties, raiding and capturing horses.

Running Eagle's End

There are conflicting accounts about the way Running Eagle died. One says she was killed in a battle. Another says she was attacked in a surprise raid. She may have died in 1840. Or 1850. Or 1860. There are frustratingly few facts on record. Still it seems likely that she died as she had lived—as a warrior.

In the mid-1800s, the US government signed a treaty with the Blackfoot Nation, allotting nearly all of what is now Montana to the tribe for hunting and dwelling. But within fifteen years, gold was discovered there, and the government promptly broke the terms of the treaty. As one newspaper baldly stated in 1865: "No one needs be told that it has become desirable to extinguish the Indian title to these lands, since nearly fifty thousand whites have settled upon them, attracted hither by the magnetic influence of the precious metals."

But the Blackfoot did not disappear. Today thousands of Blackfoot people reside in the areas where Running Eagle and her people once lived.

Lakshmibai, the Rani of Jhansi

1828–1858

The End

Most stories about a person's life begin at birth, but this one begins with death. Lakshmibai (lahk-SHMEE-bah-ee), a warrior queen, died on the battlefield wearing an Indian man's cavalry uniform after suffering a fatal wound by the sword of an unknown English soldier. She was only twenty-nine. Today she is a symbol of glory and sacrifice and is a hero in the history of India's struggle for independence from British rule. So how did she get there?

Her Training for Reigning

Lakshmibai was named Manikarnika at birth and nicknamed Manu. Her father was an important advisor to a local ruler. When Manu was only four, her mother died.

In her early years, Manu's playmates were mostly boys. (Many grew up and became leaders of the Indian independence movement.) Manu was taught to read and write, unusual for a girl in those days. She also learned how to ride a horse and to handle weapons—also unusual.

Manu was passionate, high-spirited, and intelligent. She practiced her combat skills, holding the reins in her teeth while twirling a sword in each hand. Once when one of her male playmates refused to take her for an elephant ride because she was a girl, she retorted, "I will show you! One day I will have ten elephants to your one. Remember my words!" Much later, after she became a queen,

This Seat Is Occupied

Rani is a Hindi/Sanskrit title that means "queen" or "queen-like ruler." During Lakshmibai's lifetime, India was not yet a country. Jhansi, an area in northern India, was known as a princely state, meaning it was one of many small kingdoms, and was theoretically ruled by an Indian prince. That might seem obvious—why wouldn't an Indian princely state be ruled by an Indian prince? It wasn't so simple in nineteenth-century India. At the time, more and more of the princely states were under the control of British occupiers. At first the British living in Jhansi paid little attention to Lakshmibai, the rani of Jhansi. But that lack of regard would soon change. She became one of the first Indian leaders to show Indian people that resistance was possible.

she sent that former playmate an elephant as a gift.

When Manu was only about seven, her father accepted a marriage proposal for her from a newly widowed older man named Gangadhar Rao, the raja (prince or ruler) of Jhansi. He was somewhere between forty and fifty years old, but the age difference didn't matter to him, or to Manu's father—Gangadhar Rao needed an heir, and Manu's father wanted Manu to marry well. People tended not to ask a child bride what she thought. The marriage was more of a contract—she

wouldn't have to assume official wifely duties until she was about fourteen.

After the marriage, to please her husband's family, Manu assumed the name Lakshmibai, after the Hindu goddess of wealth and victory. No less spirited than she'd been as a small child, Lakshmibai did not behave like a traditional wife or queen. As she got older, she often attended meetings with her husband and made decisions about state affairs. She stepped up her military training. She even rounded up her maid-servants and formed a small regiment of female soldiers.

Mother, Then Widow

Lakshmibai had a baby when she was twenty-three. It was a boy, and he was heir to the throne. Having a raja on deck was a relief to Lakshmibai and her husband, because British occupiers had begun taking over princely states when there was no heir. The British justified this maneuver by what they called the Doctrine of Lapse, which stated that if the line of heirs lapsed, the British got dibs on the territory. Unfortunately the baby prince died when he was only about four months old.

Soon thereafter Lakshmibai's husband fell gravely ill. One month before he died, he adopted the five-year-old son of a distant relative and renamed the child after their own dead son. Adopting an heir if your own son died was a Hindu tradition. The day before the raja died, in the presence of a British officer, he composed a letter asking British officials to recognize his adopted son as heir to the throne and to make his widow, Lakshmibai, the regent, putting her in charge until their son got older. After the raja died, his letter was ignored by British officials. They wanted to take control of Jhansi.

They did not yet understand whom they were dealing with.

The British in India

Of all the places Britain colonized in the nineteenth century, India was most prized. The British would later call it the Jewel in the Crown. The British crown, that is. Back in 1600, a group of wealthy British investors had formed a trading company, which became known as the East India Company. British merchants grew immensely wealthy from ruthlessly exploiting Indian farmers and merchants, and from trading spices, tea, cotton, and opium.

By the mid-1700s the East India Company basically controlled India. The owners acted like a government and even established an army to protect their businesses. Most of the soldiers were Indians, called sepoys. (*Sepoy* is a bad English translation of *sipahi*, the Hindi word for soldier.) The sepoys were commanded by British officers. The company made huge profits through lopsided trade deals. They ruined Indian weavers by flooding the market with cheap British-manufactured textiles, collecting taxes from Indian landowners, and seizing new territories.

For over a century, the British East India Company ruled over most of the Indian subcontinent, and the insults to Indian people mounted. English was established as the official administrative

Two Indian soldiers under the authority of the British East India company.

language. Missionaries came to convert Indian people to Christianity. Many Hindu customs were outlawed.

By the mid-1850s tensions were rising. Indian people resented the economic exploitation and the interference by the British into many customs and traditions. The tipping point came in 1856, when British officers introduced a new rifle. Rumors flew among the sepoys that the new rifle's gunpowder cartridges were lubricated with tallow—beef or pork fat. Getting the gunpowder out of the cartridge required tearing off the end of a paper with one's teeth. The majority of soldiers were either Hindus or Muslims. For Hindus, eating beef is forbidden. For Muslims, eating pork is forbidden. You see the issue.

The Revolt of 1857

Lakshmibai's problems with the company—the British governor's push to take control of Jhansi after the death of her husband—happened at the same time a rebellion was raging.

The revolt began in a town forty miles north of Delhi. Sepoys refused to obey orders, and their British commanders cracked down hard. About ninety Indian soldiers, many of them from upper-class families, were sentenced to ten years of hard labor.

The mutiny spread to other parts of northern and central India, and state after state revolted against the British. There was terrible slaughter. The revolt became known as the First War of Independence or the Great Revolution. The British called it the Sepoy Mutiny.

The Warrior Queen

In 1854 the British governor-general of India used the Doctrine of Lapse and rejected Lakshmibai's adopted child's right to the throne. Jhansi would be seized and put under direct control of the East India Company. On top of that, Lakshmibai was ordered to move out of the Jhansi fort.

The newly widowed Lakshmibai found this turn of events unacceptable. At first she tried to fight for her rights through legal channels. She visited a lawyer and filed for a hearing of her case back in London. Her appeals were ignored.

Did she give up? Of course not. For eight months she continued her campaign, writing letter after letter appealing the decision.

Lakshmibai believed she had the right to be the ruler of Jhansi, and so she stepped confidently into the role. The cleverness and bravery she'd shown since childhood now emerged in full force. She

An artist's interpretation of what Lakshmibai might have looked like.

increased her women's military unit and kept on with her own training.

Sometimes she put on male clothing. Said one British writer: "She used to dress like a man (with a turban) and rode like one."

Lakshmibai had become an embarrassment to the British East India Company. It was very bad publicity to be seen kicking a newly widowed mother of a young son out of her own home. Yet that's what happened. The British gave Lakshmibai a small pension to allow her to keep her attendants. She was removed from the fort and packed off to the Jhansi palace, where they assumed she would live in relative comfort but would give up her aspirations of ruling.

Several British officers grudgingly recorded their observations of her "extraordinary determination and forcefulness," and her "logical mind and potent intellect." Another called her "an influential and dangerous adversary."

While all this was happening, the rebellion by the sepoys was in full swing in other parts of India. As the rebels closed in on Jhansi, alarmed British officers stationed in Jhansi appealed to Lakshmibai for protection. According to some accounts, she had no wish to join the rebellion. In an effort to stave off a violent conflict, she even invited the British officers and their families to flee to the safety of her palace. But they were massacred by rebels before they could get there. She was most likely powerless to stop the marauders.

Nevertheless the British blamed Lakshmibai, and they sent reinforcements to take Jhansi. She probably knew that if she allowed British troops to enter the walls of Jhansi, she'd be arrested. And her position regarding Jhansi had not changed. It was rightfully hers.

So she decided to resist the British.

The Siege of Jhansi

Lakshmibai moved back into the fort and got her people busy preparing for battle, personally instructing her women soldiers about horseback riding and weaponry. When British soldiers laid siege to Jhansi, she and her people were ready.

British writers recounted seeing the rani riding her horse along the top of the walls of the fort, spurring on troops in her red cavalry officer uniform.

The fighting went on for about two weeks. Although outnumbered, the British soldiers were better equipped and better trained. The rani of Jhansi's forces could not keep up the resistance.

Finally the British managed to breach the walls and capture the city. Lakshmibai hoisted her adopted ten-year-old son onto her horse and tied him to her with her shawl. Then she and about three hundred soldiers escaped on horseback through a gate in the opposite wall. British troops pursued them. The two sides clashed.

After valiant fighting, Lakshmibai was mortally wounded. Her followers carried her from the battlefield and laid her in the shade of a mango tree. Just before she died, she gave orders that her soldiers should receive her jewelry.

Her adopted son was granted a pension, but Jhansi fell to the British. Like all of India, it remained under Britain's rule for nearly one hundred more years.

Lakshmibai has lived on in song and story ever since. Movies have been made about her. Nowadays Indian schoolkids learn a poem that honors her. Written by Subhadra Kumari Chauhan, a woman, the poem (in an English translation) includes the line: "outstandingly she fought, manlike, that Rani of Jhansi."

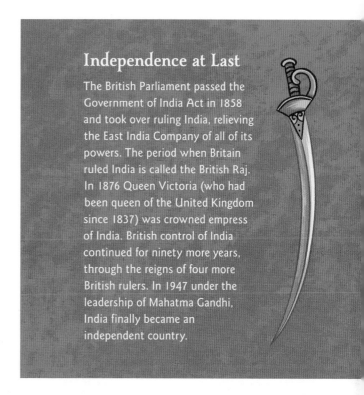

Independence at Last

The British Parliament passed the Government of India Act in 1858 and took over ruling India, relieving the East India Company of all of its powers. The period when Britain ruled India is called the British Raj. In 1876 Queen Victoria (who had been queen of the United Kingdom since 1837) was crowned empress of India. British control of India continued for ninety more years, through the reigns of four more British rulers. In 1947 under the leadership of Mahatma Gandhi, India finally became an independent country.

Amelia Bloomer

1818–1894

Hemlines Make Headlines

Amelia Bloomer published an essay in 1851 in her women's magazine, the *Lily*, about a new fashion. Amelia and a few other brave women had taken to wearing this new look in public. On top they donned a scandalously short dress—the hemline hit *well above the ankle*, almost at the shin. Underneath, more startling still, the wearer sported billowy "Turkish-style" trousers that cinched at the ankles.

Admittedly it was an odd-looking getup—picture Humpty Dumpty with a belt. But Amelia was a fan. In her essay, she spelled out why this new outfit was a good idea. It was cheaper because it required less material than the floor-length, voluminous gowns most women wore at the time. It was also more modest. (Back then *modest* was a code word for "not looking or acting like a strumpet.") Why? Because by wearing shorter dresses with trousers, a woman wouldn't have to hitch up her long skirts to cross a muddy street or to descend stairs, which often resulted in shocking glimpses of her ankles. And finally, Amelia's essay pointed out, the new outfit was more healthy and practical. The looser corset and absence of multiple petticoats allowed the wearer to breathe more freely. Women had much less weight to lug around.

In her rollicking conclusion, Amelia Bloomer argued that wearers of the new outfit should not be criticized, *especially* by anyone who "is collecting the sweepings of the sidewalk upon the hem of her dress, or who thinks it more delicate to display four-fifths of her stocking every time she crosses a street than to adopt the new dress." *Bam.* Mic drop.

Trouser Trend

The outfit Amelia Bloomer wrote about soon became known as "bloomers," but she never took credit for being the first to wear it. She stated repeatedly that she'd gotten the idea from Elizabeth "Libby" Smith Miller.

Earlier in 1851 Libby had created a stir as she strolled down the streets of Seneca Falls, New York, wearing the head-turning ensemble. She was visiting her cousin, the women's rights advocate Elizabeth Cady Stanton. Stanton happened to be a good friend of Amelia Bloomer. Soon both Elizabeth and Amelia took to wearing the new costume. And Amelia introduced Elizabeth Cady Stanton to another friend—someone you might have heard of—Susan B. Anthony. Susan also started wearing bloomers.

But Amelia was the one with her own magazine, and Bloomer was a catchy name. So the press labeled the new trend

the Bloomer Costume, and from then on the billowy trousers were known as bloomers.

A Blooming Scandal

Amelia Bloomer's essay was reprinted in newspapers all over the country. Even across the ocean in England, the story made headlines.

Hostility toward the trend was swift and vicious. Short dresses? *Trousers?* The outfit was declared a danger to the social order. It was a threat to manhood. Newspapers and magazines ran articles claiming that bloomers put all of society at risk. They printed cartoons that showed women smoking cigars and reading newspapers, while their henpecked husbands minded the baby and mopped the floor. Women who dared to wear the outfit in public drew jeers and laughter on the street. People threw sticks and stones.

Amelia seemed to not mind all the kerfuffle. It helped publicize her magazine and the cause for women's rights. She and her fellow activists continued to wear bloomers. Letters of support from women all over the country poured into the offices at the *Lily.* Many asked for a pattern—a paper template of the garment that could be traced onto fabric, cut out, and sewn at home.

What Women Wore

Imagine you're a girl from a well-off family in 1850, and it's time to get dressed. It's cold, and your house isn't heated, so the quicker you can get into your clothes, the better. Start with a bath? Uh, no. There's no hot water.

The floor is icy cold, so pull on your woolen socks first. They roll up and over your knees. Next come your pantalets. (In genteel society you would call them "inexpressibles.") They tie at the waist and reach just below your knee.

Next pull off your billowy nightdress and quickly pull on a cotton chemise, which will keep your corset from chafing your skin too much. That's right: the corset is next, and it has to be laced up, cinched, and tied tightly. Next comes your wool-and-horsehair petticoat. It's heavy and itchy, but it'll keep you warm. A cotton petticoat goes over that. Then another—this one with whalebone or stiffeners sewn into the seams and padded below the knee—to fluff out your dress. Then a starched white petticoat with flounces, a muslin underskirt, and finally your gown. There are a whole lot of tiny buttons (or hooks and eyes) from your neck all the way down to your waist. If your dress buttons up the back, you will need an assistant to help. Oh, wait. Forgot about the boots. You should have put those on first, because now that you're in your corset and your fitted dress, you can only bend stiffly at the waist to get those laced up. Finally it's time for accessories: hair ribbons, bonnet, parasol, fan, shawl, gloves, and jewelry.

Ready to stagger off to face the day? You're now lugging around fifteen to twenty-five extra pounds. And you can't raise your arms above your head. Also you may need to change your outfit three or four more times today—you wear different outfits for walking, riding horses, teatime, and evening dining.

A casual family outing in not-so-casual clothing.

A staged photo showing what might happen if husbands let their wives wear pants.

Amelia traveled all over in her bloomer outfit, speaking about temperance (not drinking alcohol) and women's rights. She didn't seem to mind if some people came just to gawk at her clothes. "If the dress drew the crowds that came to hear me it was well. They heard the message I brought them, and it has borne abundant fruit."

In the time-honored tradition of being embarrassed by your parents, many of the bloomer wearers' kids were ashamed to be seen with their mothers. When Elizabeth Cady Stanton's son wrote home from his boarding school, he begged her not to visit him dressed in the bloomer outfit.

Amelia Bloomer's mission was about so much more than what to wear. At the *Lily*, she hired a woman typesetter—a first. The other typesetters—all male—protested and threatened to walk out. Amelia gave them a chance to change their minds, but they were firm in their resolve not to work with a woman. So she sacked them all and hired four more women and three new men who didn't object to working alongside them.

Moving On

After several years of wearing bloomers and speaking about voting rights, education, and temperance, Amelia moved with her supportive husband, Dexter C. Bloomer, to Ohio, and then to Council Bluffs, Iowa. The winds in Iowa were so strong, they sometimes blew her skirts up over her head. She tried sewing lead weights into the hemline, but her skirt banged against her legs and bruised them. So she stopped wearing the bloomer costume.

Luckily Amelia's return to long skirts coincided with the invention of a lighter-weight, collapsible steel hoop cage. The hoops helped women achieve a poofed-out skirt without having to wear multiple heavy petticoats. And by the 1860s, thanks to the invention of the sewing machine, it became possible to sew a dress with a hemline almost seven feet in diameter in a previously inconceivably short amount of time. The bloomer costume vanished from the scene. For a while. But several decades later, Amelia Bloomer's bloomers made a comeback. All thanks to . . . the bicycle.

Legally His

In 1850 women who were citizens of the United States had few rights in the eyes of the law. (Enslaved women had none.) Women in most states couldn't vote. Women who worked outside the home had limited choices for jobs and were paid a fraction of what men made for doing the same work.

As soon as a woman married, she lost all her stuff. Any money or property she owned became her husband's. The law also granted her husband any wages she earned and the children she gave birth to.

Prevailing attitudes about women's rights are spelled out clearly in a book of that era called *The Introduction to American Law*, which says, "The legal theory is, marriage makes the husband and wife one person, and that person is the husband. There is scarcely a legal act of any description that she is competent to perform."

By the late 1800s, society began to accept the "new woman" who wore bloomers to ride a bike.

A Vicious Cycle (If You're Wearing a Skirt)

Early versions of the bicycle had been invented at the beginning of the 1800s, but they were heavy and difficult to ride. Around mid-century, steel-wheeled versions appeared. They were called bone-shakers. In the 1880s, "high-mounters" were popular. They had huge front wheels and required a lot of coordination. And forget about trying to ride one if you were wearing a long skirt.

In the 1890s the safety bicycle arrived. It looked a lot like modern bikes, with better tires and brakes than its predecessors. A bicycle craze struck. For the first time a woman could travel from place to place without a man. She had wheels!

As more and more women began tootling around on bicycles, the debate about proper attire returned. At first women tried to ride while wearing their long skirts, but the skirts became tangled in the wheels, resulting in many disastrous accidents.

More and more enthusiastic female cyclists took to wearing "rational dress," donning bloomers and knickerbockers and even, for the truly daring, actual trousers. Amelia Bloomer, by then in her seventies, was delighted to see the reappearance of her radical outfit.

As had Amelia and other early bloomer wearers, many women cyclists endured jeering and hostile crowds. Some were even arrested for indecency and causing a disturbance on a public street. In 1898 a woman cyclist in New York City was taken into police custody, "charged with having masqueraded on the Boulevard on Thursday night in male attire." She'd been wearing trousers, along with "a stiff shirt and a cutaway coat and a dicky collar, and her hair was tucked away under a man's hat." That indecent getup earned her a night in the pokey.

Gradually, though, people got used to the newfangled bicycle outfits, and outrage became bemused curiosity and then admiration. As one Chicago paper put it, "The fashionable girl no longer lolls about in tea gowns in darkened rooms, but joins her male friends for a spin in a fetching sailor hat, a shirtwaist with a mannish collar, leg-o'-mutton sleeves, and bloomers." In 1898 a San Francisco newspaper gushed that "Bicycle dresses were bizarre two years ago and last season they were not much better. But the bicycle styles this year are all that can be desired. They are really beautiful creations, such as one would not hesitate to wear anywhere."

Turns out that Amelia Bloomer, who died in 1894, was way ahead of her time.

Harriet Tubman

ABOUT 1820–1913

Harriet the Spy

You've probably heard of Harriet Tubman. She's most famous for her brave rescues, helping enslaved people escape by fleeing north in the days before the Civil War. She herself escaped from slavery in 1849, traveling from Maryland to Philadelphia through ninety miles of forests, fields, rivers, and swamps. And then, again and again and again, she snuck back to rescue others, confounding and enraging white slaveholders.

Over ten years she risked her own life by making as many as nineteen trips and rescuing at least seventy enslaved people—some accounts put the number closer to three hundred. She was often called Moses, after the man in the Bible who led his people to freedom.

But did you know that Harriet Tubman was also a war hero? Soldiers, both Black and white, called her General Tubman. Who was this woman who was known by two different male nicknames and who often cross-dressed to get the job done?

By the time the Civil War began, in 1861, Harriet was famous in the North and a notorious outlaw in the South. An admirer and abolitionist (an antislavery activist) named John Brown described her as "one of the bravest persons on this continent," and "the most of a man, naturally, that I ever met with."

In 1863 President Lincoln issued a proclamation that would eventually free most slaves. Soon afterward Black soldiers were permitted to join the Union Army (otherwise known as the US army, or the Northern army). Harriet joined the Union cause. She worked first as a nurse, and then as a scout and a spy in South Carolina.

During the war, her proven talents for learning and remembering critical information paid off, as did her skills at deception, acting, and predicting human behavior. She crept into enemy territory and pretended to be an enslaved woman. She befriended enslaved people who worked for Confederate (Southern) commanders. They informed her of Confederate troop movements and battle plans. She passed along the information to Union generals from her network of agents.

Perhaps her greatest triumph happened in June 1863. Harriet planned and helped carry out a massive raid near the Combahee River in South Carolina. At several large plantations close to the river, Confederate troops were stocking food and supplies and holding hundreds of enslaved people. Confederate troops had laid mines below the surface of the river, so if any boat passed it would explode. But Harriet knew about rivers. She and her scouts figured out where the mines were, and she helped the Union warships navigate around them. The Union troops, including a regiment of Black soldiers, attacked the plantations. In the process, Harriet helped more than 750 enslaved people—including women, children, and infants—into small boats that transported them to Union ships and freedom. The mission was a success, thanks largely to Harriet and her spy network. An official Confederate report later stated: "The enemy seems to have been well posted as to the character and capacity of our troops and their small chance of encountering opposition, and to have been well guided by persons thoroughly acquainted with the river and country."

In the frenzy of the rescue, Harriet tried to help a woman carrying two squealing pigs onboard a boat. Recounting the incident in a letter later, Harriet described how she had stepped on the hem of her own long skirt, and "tore it almost off, so that when I got on board the boat, there was hardly anything else but shreds." She vowed to never again wear a skirt for military work. She requested "a bloomer dress, made of some coarse, strong material, to wear on expeditions."

Harriet became the first woman ever to help plan and carry out a military operation in the United States. She also proved that Black soldiers were effective soldiers. No wonder they called her General Tubman.

Enslaved people fleeing to safety during Harriet's raid near the Combahee River.

Early Life

Harriet was born into slavery as Araminta "Minty" Ross on a farm in Maryland around 1820. Her parents were named Benjamin and Harriet—Minty later changed her first name to Harriet after her mother. She had eight brothers and sisters. Harriet's three oldest siblings were sold away to a plantation deep in the South, and the family lost touch with them forever.

When Harriet was only five or six, she was hired out to nearby families as a house servant. These other families whipped and beat her frequently. As she grew older and stronger, she began working outside more, checking animal traps in streams and rivers and working as a field hand.

When Harriet was in her twenties, she married a man named John Tubman. He was a free Black man, but Harriet remained enslaved. She took his last name as her own.

When Harriet was almost thirty, the plantation owner died. Soon after that, a slave trader appeared on the farm, and

Harriet Tubman a few years after the end of the war, back in a dress.

Harriet caught wind of a rumor that she and two of her brothers would be sold. It was time to run. Harriet's husband did not want to go with her, but her brothers did. Soon after they set out, though, fearing they'd be caught and punished, her brothers turned back. Harriet reluctantly returned too, but not long after that she ran again, this time on her own.

The Flight

Details of Harriet's first flight are sketchy, but we know she traveled mostly at night. Her father had taught her how to find her way by following the North Star. On cloudy nights, she knew how to feel for moss on trees, which grew on the north side of the trunk. She followed a river that wound mostly northward.

She also had help from a secret network known as the Underground Railroad. It wasn't an actual railroad. It was a group of people who hid runaway slaves and helped them move from one safe location to another until they could cross the border into the North. The network included mostly enslaved people and free Black people, but also some white Quakers and other abolitionists. A local woman whispered to Harriet one day, giving her instructions to a farm in Delaware forty miles north, where people would be waiting to help her to the next

Tactics

Harriet Tubman had never been allowed to learn to read, but she had an amazing visual memory. She seemed to be able to create imaginary maps in her head, learning terrain, the course of rivers, and different roads. The skills would prove invaluable during the war. She also came up with ingenious strategies to avoid detection. She often set off with escaping slaves on a Saturday night, knowing that ads for their return would not appear in newspapers until Monday. Because wanted posters showed her as a small woman with a scar on her forehead, she sometimes disguised herself as a man and wore a hat to hide her scar. She often instructed her charges to wear disguises too. She asked men to wear women's clothes and women to wear men's clothes.

She brought medicine along that made babies sleep so their cries wouldn't give away the group. Members of her secret network sang spiritual songs that sent coded messages to others. She even carried a gun, which could come in handy in case the escapees were overtaken by a bounty hunter or bloodhound. She didn't hesitate to use it to threaten members of the group who lost their nerve or decided they were too tired to continue the grueling journey. Were they to turn back, they might be forced to divulge the whereabouts of everyone else. Harriet coolly informed them they'd be shot before she let them go back. It worked.

THREE HUNDRED DOLLARS REWARD.

RANAWAY from the subscriber on Monday the 17th ult., three negroes, named as follows: HARRY, aged about 19 years, has on one side of his neck a wen, just under the ear, he is of a dark chestnut color, about 5 feet 8 or 9 inches hight; BEN, aged aged about 25 years, is very quick to speak when spoken to, he is of a chestnut color, about six feet high; MINTY, aged about 27 years, is of a chestnut color, fine looking, and about 5 feet high. One hundred dollars reward will be given for each of the above named negroes, if taken out of the State, and $50 each if taken in the State. They must be lodged in Baltimore, Easton or Cambridge Jail, in Maryland.

ELIZA ANN BRODESS.
Near Bucktown, Dorchester county, Md.
Oct. 3d, 1849.

☞The Delaware Gazette will please copy the above three weeks, and charge this office.

The notice that Harriet (Minty), Ben, and Harry had escaped. After a few weeks, her brothers turned back, but Harriet tried again and succeeded.

"station." In Delaware, the farmer smuggled her to Wilmington in the back of his wagon. The next helper gave her a set of men's clothes and instructed her to act like one of his workmen. She trudged into town behind him, a shovel over her shoulder, pretending to be a man as if her life depended on it, which it did. No one paid any attention. At the next stop, she was told how to follow signposts pointing to Pennsylvania, which was a free state. Once over the state line, it wasn't far to the city of Philadelphia.

There, abolitionists helped her find work and also helped her meet other abolitionists and members of the Underground Railroad. She saved her money, determined to rescue her family and other loved ones. A year later she made her first trip back into Maryland. She'd begun as a passenger on the Underground Railroad. But now she was a conductor—and would become the best of all time.

Helping Others

Time and again Harriet went back to rescue family members—sisters, brothers, nieces, and nephews. On her third trip, she went in search of her husband, John Tubman. But he had remarried and did not want to go. Although she was at first distressed by his rejection, Harriet quickly found ten other people to help and guided the group safely north.

In 1857 she even managed to rescue her seventy-year-old parents under extremely risky conditions. They were not well enough to walk long distances. So Harriet took a train south in broad daylight. Somehow she evaded capture, bought a horse, fashioned a carriage, and helped to get them all the way to Canada.

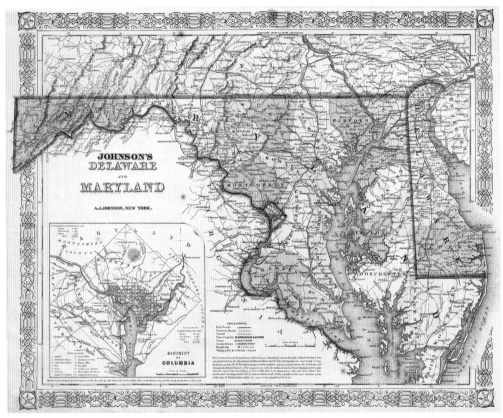

This Civil War–era map shows the boundary between Northern and Southern states: the Mason–Dixon line.

Later Life

After the war was over, Harriet settled in Auburn, New York, where she had relocated her aging parents, and opened her home to many other people. It was a constant struggle to pay the bills, because after the Union won the Civil War, the US government did not pay her for her wartime service.

A woman named Sarah Bradford wrote Harriet's biography, which became a popular book. Sarah gave Harriet all the money it earned, which helped pay at least some of Harriet's expenses. It wasn't until 1899 that Harriet was finally awarded some official recognition. She received a small pension. And when she died, at age ninety-three, she was given a military funeral.

Rosa Bonheur

1822–1899

Dress Distress

A French artist named Rosa Bonheur received special permission in 1857 from the French police to wear men's clothing without being arrested.

Women in France had been prohibited from dressing in men's clothing for more than half a century. The law allowed an exception only if a woman could present medical evidence that she had some sort of unusual condition—say, if she had a full beard—that made wearing pants necessary. The only time that the law was *not* strictly enforced was during Carnival, the wild, anything-goes holiday celebration leading up to Lent. At all other times, women who broke the law could be fined and jailed. A woman who dressed as a man was considered immoral, an outrage against nature, a threat to men, and most likely a harlot.

Besides the no-pants law, French custom prohibited respectable ladies from leaving the house alone without a male escort. Conservative-minded citizens generally agreed that women were unfit to take on tasks traditionally performed by men, such as politics, fighting in wars, and having jobs. In their view, respectable women belonged inside—in skirts of course—where they were expected to concern themselves with home and family. Nor could a proper woman smoke in public or go riding astride her horse (as opposed to sidesaddle). If a woman took up painting as a hobby, she was expected to paint stuff like fruit in bowls or flowers in vases—whatever she could find inside her home. She should certainly not venture outside and set up her easel wherever she wanted.

Rosa Bonheur was not the sort of person to obey customs and laws if she thought they were dumb. She dressed in pants, smoked in public, and rode astride. She painted outside, often in rough-and-tumble places where few women went. And she never married, declaring, "I wed art. It is my husband, my world, my life's dream, the air I breathe."

She became not just a famous painter but a rich one too.

An Unusual School

Rosa's real name was Marie-Rosalie Bonheur. She was the oldest of four kids, with two brothers and a sister. She was born in a part of France called Bordeaux. Rosa's father, Raymond, was an artist who made a meager living teaching art. Her mother, Sophie, was a piano teacher. The family was not well off. When Rosa was about six, her father moved to Paris in order to make more money. He missed his family terribly, and he and Rosa's mother wrote each other often.

When Rosa was about seven, the family joined Raymond in Paris. They moved frequently from one shabby neighborhood to another. Paris had grand museums where a budding young artist could get a great art education, and sprawling parks, where an animal lover could explore nature.

Rosa loathed school. Her mother coaxed her to learn to read by having her draw an animal to represent each letter of the alphabet. Rosa later said that this early exercise led to her lifelong love of painting animals.

Along with the rest of her siblings, she received early painting and sculpture training from her father. When she was about ten, her father joined a religious group called the Saint-Simonians. According to their beliefs, God was both male and female. Saint-Simonians believed in equality between men and women, a notion that was extremely forward-thinking for that time. And they believed that this equality could partly be expressed through what they wore. Both men and women wore trousers. Rosa attended school alongside boys, which was also unusual for that time.

Rosa's mother died when Rosa was only eleven, from what appears to have been sheer exhaustion. As Rosa's biographer later wrote, Rosa's mother was "prematurely worn out by the trials of a precarious life."

Painting for Pennies, Fooling at School

When Rosa was about twelve, her father tried to send her out as an apprentice to a dressmaker. She hated it. Back home she went.

At last some friends of her father gave Rosa a job she loved. The Bissons were a married couple who made a living painting family heralds, which were sort of like a fancy family's personal logo. She helped paint heralds to earn a few cents. Madame Bisson treated her like a daughter. As Rosa later wrote, "Mother of three boys and inconsolable at having no girls, she had rebaptised her sons with girls' names. The youngest, who was my friend, was called Eleanor."

When Rosa got a bit older, her father sent her to a boarding school run by a woman named Madame Gilbert. Rosa was soon pegged as a troublemaker. She amused her classmates by cutting out "grotesque figures in paper, tying them with a bit of thread to a lump of chewed bread, and then throwing them up to the ceiling, where they dangled and cut capers to the delight of the class and the scandal of the principal." One day she fashioned some wooden swords and challenged some kids to a pretend sword fight. As Rosa later recounted, "I ordered a cavalry charge. The result was the destruction of Mme. Gilbert's fine rose-bed which was her pride." She got kicked out of school.

Plowing in Nivernais, one of Rosa Bonheur's most famous paintings.

Born to Paint

One day Rosa's father returned from work and found Rosa putting the finishing touches on a painting of a cluster of cherries. He was astounded by her skill. Although he'd initially been reluctant to encourage his daughter to live an artist's life, he recognized her talent and determination and trained her in earnest. While her brothers and sister went to school, Rosa stayed in her father's studio. In the morning before he left for work, he gave her a task—something to paint or engrave—and in the evening he would inspect and critique it. Eventually she took to going to the Louvre, a famous Paris museum, and copying images from master paintings. She got better and better.

When Rosa was a teenager, she realized her true passion was painting animals. She loved to escape to the countryside to paint them in their natural surroundings. She kept rabbits, birds, a goat, a squirrel, finches, canaries, and even a sheep named Jocrisse. Every day Rosa's brother hoisted Jocrisse onto his shoulders and carried her down six flights of stairs to graze.

Early in her career, Rosa dressed in a painter's smock and pants when she went out painting by herself in fields and farms. She spent long days at slaughterhouses, horse fairs, and farmers' markets to paint working animals like dogs, horses, and oxen. She later said that in the rough atmosphere of the slaughterhouses, where the workers were all men, it was much safer and more practical to wear trousers. She also kept a pistol in her pocket.

All this hard work paid off. She began to sell her paintings. At nineteen, Rosa had her first exhibition. Two of her pictures, *Goats and Sheep* and *Rabbits Nibbling Carrots*, were shown at a famous French art exhibition called the Salon. Both were well received, so the next year she sent three more. She continued to exhibit at the Salon and won four medals. When she was only twenty-seven, her painting of some oxen won a gold medal.

Her most successful painting was a huge work called *The Horse Fair*. Printed copies of it sold well, especially in England, and she made enough money to buy a large estate outside Paris, in a town called Fontainebleau. In her country home she kept a small zoo that included ponies, deer, monkeys, cattle, and even a young lion. She lived there for forty years with her friend, Nathalie. After Nathalie died, Rosa, who was in her seventies, lived with a much younger woman, an American painter named Anna. Anna helped Rosa write an autobiography.

In 1865 she received the prestigious Legion of Honor medal from the French

Rosa Bonheur.

empress Eugenie. Rosa was the first woman ever to receive such an honor.

The more famous she got, the more often Rosa wore full-on male attire. She cut her hair short and smoked in public. Perhaps it was a way to increase acceptance by the all-male world of Parisian artists or to show that she was their equal. Or perhaps it's just how she liked to dress.

The Law at Long Last Is Lifted

When Rosa received official permission from French authorities in 1857 to "dress as a man," it was granted for "health reasons," presumably because the law conceded that Rosa needed trousers and thick boots to tromp around the farms and cattle pens where she painted. She'd been dressing as she pleased for years, but now that she was famous, the government made her permission official and permanent. The permit noted that Rosa's permission to dress in men's clothes did not apply to "shows, balls, and other meeting events open to the public."

Rosa continued to dress as she pleased until she died, in 1899. She was seventy-eight.

The French law forbidding women to wear trousers was ignored by lady bicyclists during the bicycle craze of the 1890s, when throngs of female riders wore trousers or knickers. Ten years after Rosa's death, in 1909, officials changed the law to permit a woman to wear "divided skirts" if she "holds in her hand the handlebars of a bicycle or the reins of a horse."

A few years later World War I began. Women took jobs in factories and offices to replace the men who'd gone off to fight, and they put on pants to perform the work. By then French authorities had given up trying to enforce the law. From that point on it was basically ignored.

The law was finally revoked . . . in 2013.

Rosa Bonheur may have helped women realize that it should be a basic human right, whether legal or not, for a person to dress as she pleases.

The Scandalous George Sand

There's another French woman who famously dressed in men's clothes and who lived at roughly the same time as Rosa Bonheur. She went by the name of George Sand. Rosa was a great admirer of hers.

George Sand, who was born Amantine-Aurore-Lucile Dupin, wrote more than one hundred novels; a massive multivolume autobiography; seventeen plays; and countless short stories, letters, and essays. She cared deeply about women's rights and wrote essays protesting unfair laws that denied women the right to own property or escape an abusive husband. In France, George Sand is known as the most famous woman writer of the nineteenth century. Elsewhere she is also remembered for her nine-year love affair with the composer Frédéric Chopin.

Early in her career as a writer, George Sand strolled through the streets of Paris smoking cigars and dressed in men's clothes. She believed that her male disguise allowed her to observe people without being observed herself, to go places where unescorted women rarely ventured (like the theater), and to collect ideas for her writing. "No one knew me, no one looked at me, no one stopped me," she later said. After she became famous, she continued to wear men's clothing. Her attire did not go over well with stodgy critics. As one man wrote, "What the deuce, then, could Mme. Sand be doing when she put on breeches . . . ? After all, perhaps, it was simply so as to be the better able to gad about!"

Well, yeah.

George Sand.

Ellen Craft

1826–1891

Crafty Costume

Early in the morning of December 12, 1848, a slight, sickly-looking young white gentleman arrived at a train station in Macon, Georgia. He bought two tickets, one for himself and one for his enslaved manservant. The train was bound for Savannah, Georgia, roughly two hundred miles east. The young man's right arm was in a sling. His jaw was bound in a bandage and tied at the top of his head, suggesting that he had a terrible tooth-ache. He wore green-tinted spectacles, as though the light bothered his eyes. He directed his enslaved servant to stow the luggage, and then he boarded a first-class train car. His servant, a dark-skinned man in his mid-twenties, had to sit in a car designated for Black people.

The young white man settled in at a window seat as the train moved out of the station. An older white man entered and sat down, wishing the younger man "a very fine morning." No reply. The second man repeated his greeting, but again received no reply. Was the younger man hard of hearing?

"I will make him hear!" the second man said, and bellowed, "It is a very fine morning, sir!"

At last the young man turned stiffly, muttered a "yes," and went back to looking out the window. The older man turned in amusement to the other passengers in the car and loudly announced that he would "not trouble that fellow any more." The rest of the passengers chatted among themselves until the train got to the next stop, where the older man got off.

As it turned out, the bandaged-up young man could hear just fine. And he wasn't ill. Nor was he even a young man. She was a young *woman*, and her real name was Ellen Craft. Ellen was a light-skinned enslaved woman about twenty-two years old. She was disguised as a wealthy white man.

She was also, in that moment, utterly terrified, because she knew the older guy who'd sat down next to her. He was good friends with the man who enslaved her, Robert Collins. The man had known her for most of her life and had just had dinner at the Collinses' house the night before. Luckily the green-tinted glasses she wore had hidden the panicky expression in her eyes, and the man hadn't recognized her.

And who was the enslaved man who had boarded the train with Ellen? His name was William Craft, and he was her husband. Together they were embarking on a bold—some would say foolhardy—plan to escape slavery and flee to the North, a journey of more than a thousand miles.

Born in the Deep South

Ellen was born in 1826, in Clinton, Georgia—deep in the southeastern part of the United States. Her mother was an enslaved Black woman named Maria. Ellen's father, James Smith, was a white lawyer. He owned Maria. Besides Ellen's mother, he also owned about a hundred other people.

James Smith was married to a white woman named Eliza. Together they had five children. Besides Ellen, it's not certain how many other children he fathered with enslaved women against their will.

Because both Ellen and her mother worked as house servants, Ellen had the chance to observe and learn the manners and speech of wealthy white people from Georgia. That would come in handy later.

As a young child Ellen played with her half siblings, both Black and white. Because she had pale skin and straight hair, visitors to the plantation often mistakenly assumed that Ellen was one of Eliza's own children. Awkward. Through no fault of Ellen's, she was a reminder to Eliza of her husband's deplorable behavior.

When Ellen was eleven, Eliza gave her away to her daughter, also named Eliza, as a wedding present. Imagine giving a human being to someone as a gift, like a fish platter or a punch bowl. But it happened all the time.

So now young Ellen was the property of her own half sister. She was brought to Macon, Georgia, to live with

Eliza and her new husband, Robert Collins. In Georgia it was against the law to educate a slave, so Ellen had not learned how to read or write. But she was an excellent seamstress. She became her half sister's maidservant, helping her get dressed and probably sleeping outside her bedroom door.

Ellen Meets William

In Macon, Ellen met her future husband, William Craft. He was enslaved by a different owner.

A trained cabinetmaker and a skilled carpenter, William was able to earn a little extra money for himself, and he saved it carefully. Soon he would need it.

Before long, he and Ellen fell in love, and in 1846 they asked permission to be married. Even though marriages between enslaved people weren't considered legal, couples still had to get permission to have a ceremony. Ellen and William were allowed to wed. Ellen did not want to have children, because of the anguish she knew it would cause her. Any children she and William had would belong to Ellen's owner. As a boy, William had seen most of his own family sold off. Neither one of them could bear the idea of seeing their children sold away. They discussed running away many times. But this was Georgia, a thousand miles from a free

Ellen in disguise.

state. Few enslaved people managed to elude bloodhounds and bounty hunters over such a vast distance. Famous fugitives such as Harriet Tubman and Frederick Douglass had been enslaved in states much farther north.

The Daring Plan

After they'd been married for two years, William and Ellen finally hatched their bold plan. Ellen would disguise herself as a sick white gentleman named Mr. Johnson. Mr. Johnson would say he was heading to Philadelphia for medical treatment. William, whose skin was much darker than Ellen's, would pose as

Mr. Johnson's enslaved manservant. They considered, but dismissed, the idea of Ellen posing as a white *woman*. It would have been improper for a woman to travel alone with a male servant. Because Ellen couldn't read or write, she tied her right arm in a sling so she wouldn't be expected to sign their names in registers along the way. The bandage around her chin would hide the fact that she had no whisker stubble. It was a genius idea. And yet think how terrifying it must have been to run away in broad daylight, right beneath the noses of the people who most wanted them caught.

Because William's carpentry work permitted him some freedom to move around without attracting suspicion, he was able to purchase Ellen's outfit, including boots, a frock coat, and a top hat. Ellen sewed her own trousers. Christmas was approaching, and they decided that would be a good time to flee. Because they were trusted, both received written permission to visit friends in the countryside for a few days. It was against the law for slaves to travel on boats or trains without proper papers. The pretend visit would give them a few days' head start before anyone noticed they hadn't returned.

On the night before their escape, William cut Ellen's hair short. The next morning, just before dawn, she donned her disguise. Soon after, the two left for the train station.

The Perilous Journey

There was no direct train from Macon, Georgia, to Philadelphia, Pennsylvania. The harrowing four-day journey would require multiple train changes, overnight stays, carriage rides, and steamships. They would be forced to interact with stationmasters, hotel clerks, and nosy white people.

After that first terrifying train ride from Macon to Savannah, where Ellen managed to avoid being recognized by the Collins family friend, she and William boarded a horse-drawn omnibus that took them to the wharves in Savannah. There they boarded a steamship bound for Charleston, South Carolina. In Charleston, they took a boat to Wilmington, North Carolina, and then a train to Richmond, Virginia. Then another train, a smaller steamer, yet another train to Baltimore, and finally, a train to Philadelphia. Travel was not easy back then, even if you *weren't* running for your life and wearing a conspicuous disguise.

Time and again during their journey, they faced perils. On the ship bound for Charleston, Ellen pretended to be ill so she could retire to her room and not have

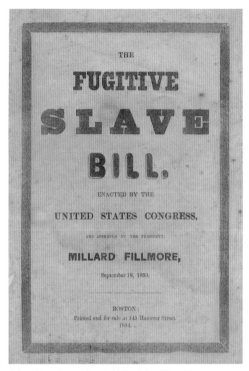

A booklet about the 1850 Fugitive Slave Act.

A Terrible New Law

In 1850 Congress passed a law called the Fugitive Slave Act. President Millard Fillmore supported it. According to the law, anyone helping escaped slaves—even in a Northern free state—would be subject to a thousand-dollar fine and six months in jail.

Formerly enslaved people who had fled to Northern states were no longer safe. According to the new law, they could be captured and returned to their owners in the South no matter where they were. Professional slave hunters chased down fugitives who had fled north and returned them in exchange for quite a lot of money.

to smoke cigars and drink brandy with the other white men. At breakfast the next morning, a white passenger reprimanded Ellen-as-Mr. Johnson for saying "please" and "thank you" to William.

They stayed overnight at a fancy hotel in Charleston, where the staff fawned over "Mr. Johnson." The next morning, at the customs house, the man behind the counter insisted that Ellen sign a document testifying that William belonged to her. The man didn't care that her arm was in a sling and would have

difficulty signing. She must sign anyway. After all, there were strict regulations about taking enslaved people out of state. Luckily a white man who had been with them on the ship from Savannah stepped out of line, agreed to vouch for them, and signed the register for Ellen.

On the train to Richmond, a white man traveling with two grown daughters gave Ellen a recipe to help with rheumatism. Ellen nodded thanks and hastily tucked it away. She didn't dare pretend to read it, because she didn't know how and might hold it upside down and give herself away. The daughters flirted with Ellen, believing her to be an eligible single gentleman in need of a wife.

Ellen and William Craft.

On the final leg of the journey, they had their worst scare. At the train station, William was stopped by the conductor and told to fetch his master. They were directed to go to the railway office to provide documents that proved that William was indeed owned by Mr. Johnson. They were at the border between Maryland, a slave state, and Pennsylvania, a free state. Abolitionists had been trying to smuggle slaves across the border to freedom by posing as slave owners. Of course William and Ellen had no such documents. But Ellen's careful observations from years of living in the Smith and Collins houses

paid off. She played the part of the imperious privileged gentleman talking to an underling and demanded that they be allowed to board. Then the bell rang, signaling that the train was about to leave. The intimidated clerk, clearly not willing to get himself in trouble by causing this important man to miss his train, permitted them to board.

As soon as the train crossed the border into Pennsylvania, they realized they were finally free. As they got off the train and walked away from the station, Ellen burst into tears and said, "Thank God, William, we're safe!"

Freedom

They went straight to the home of an abolitionist. That person sent them on to Boston. They lived there for two years and both learned to read and write. Ellen managed to make a good living as a seamstress. William had more of a struggle to find work as a cabinetmaker, because people up North were nearly as racist as those down South.

Abolitionists encouraged the Crafts to give speeches about their ordeal. Their escape story was published in many newspapers, and they became famous. Newspapers down South also carried the story. Ellen's former owner read it—and issued warrants for their arrest.

Fame and a Family, Finally

One day two men came to Boston, determined to find the Crafts and bring them back to Georgia. Word of the slave hunters' arrival spread among antislavery people, and the two men were hounded everywhere they went. They were arrested multiple times for small offenses such as smoking on the street and driving a carriage too fast. But proslavery people kept paying to bail them out. When President Millard Fillmore declared that he would send soldiers to Boston to enforce the Fugitive Slave Act, the Crafts' abolitionist friends raised funds and sent Ellen and William off to England, where slavery had been abolished in 1833. They lived there for nineteen years. William published a book about their escape, and the two traveled around speaking to audiences about it.

The Crafts remained free for the rest of their lives. They had five children. Ellen was able to send funds to buy her mother's freedom, and her mother joined them in England. In 1868, with slavery abolished throughout the United States, the Crafts returned without fear of being arrested. They had been away for twenty years. They purchased an old plantation and opened a school for Southern Black children. Still, life remained a struggle, as many of the laws at the time made it difficult for Black people to make a living. But the story of the Crafts' daring escape inspired untold numbers of people to fight for their own freedom.

Lozen

ABOUT 1840-1889

On the Run

One day in 1880, a woman named Lozen stood on the banks of the Rio Grande on the border of Texas and Mexico. Lozen belonged to an Apache tribe. Lozen watched her brother, Victorio, and the rest of her group ride away, heading west toward Mexico. Victorio was the leader of this group of Chihenne Apache (also known as Warm Springs), and they had been on the run from US government soldiers for three years. Lozen had been at her brother's side the whole time and was considered one of the bravest fighters in Victorio's group.

Next to Lozen on the riverbank was a young woman named Eclode. Eclode was very pregnant and ready to give birth. Lozen had volunteered to stay behind and help bring the baby into the world. Eclode was a Mescalero Apache. She wanted to get back to the reservation, in what today is part of New Mexico, where the Mescalero people lived and where she and her baby would be relatively safe. Lozen knew they faced a journey of many weeks, and it would not be easy. There was a harsh desert to cross, and soldiers were everywhere.

Lozen's Childhood

Lozen had never been interested in the traditional roles of Apache women. As a young girl, she had learned to ride horses and use weapons. She often won footraces against boys her age. She had gained the respect of her people, and she was invited to partake in a sacred ceremony usually reserved for boys. According to oral accounts, the mountain spirits granted her sacred powers, most notably the ability to sense an enemy's location. Whether or not she actually had supernatural powers, she certainly had a ghostlike ability to help her group elude soldiers.

"Lozen is as my right hand," Victorio once declared. "Strong as a man, braver than most, and cunning in strategy. Lozen is a shield to her people." She was also great at roping horses and cattle. "No man in the tribe was more skillful in stealing horses or stampeding a herd," her nephew later said.

The Birth

Almost as soon as Victorio and the rest of the group had left, Eclode's labor pains started. Lozen knew they had to find a hiding place. She helped the mother-to-be turn off the path, but they couldn't get very far. Poor Eclode, in the throes of labor, knew she must not cry out.

Lozen helped deliver the baby. It was a boy. She said a prayer for him and swaddled him in a bit of blanket that Eclode had brought with her. Lozen cut some willow shoots and bent them into a cradle.

Then she turned to the next problem at hand: they needed food and water. And they had nothing to carry the water in. She spotted some cattle drinking at the river, but she couldn't risk firing a shot, because patrolling soldiers might hear it. According to one Apache historian, "Killing a longhorn with a knife is a feat that few men would undertake, but Lozen did it. She cut the strips of the meat and carried it to their retreat."

Did you get that? She crept up on a cow the size of a minivan sporting pointy horns six feet across, and killed it *with a knife*. She cut away as much meat as she could carry, and then returned to their hiding place to dry it out so they could stash away some provisions.

Next they needed a horse. Lozen cut a narrow strip of hide from the dead longhorn and tied it to her belt. She'd use that as a bridle. At nightfall, she crept down to the river. Earlier she had spotted a camp of Mexican cavalry soldiers on the Mexican side of the river. She plunged in and swam across.

The camp was about half a mile upstream where the riverbank sloped steeply upward. Lozen hid and waited for the soldiers to go to sleep. Finally, they all retired except for one, who stood guard. The horses were hobbled, meaning their legs were bound with rope so they couldn't run off.

From where she hid, Lozen chose the horse she wanted. When the guard wandered toward the campfire, she stole forward and threw her homemade bridle around her chosen horse. But as she stooped to cut away the hobble ropes, another horse snorted and reared. Lozen knew she had no time to lose. She leaped onto the horse—bareback of course—and galloped toward the river.

That woke the soldiers up.

With bullets whizzing around them, Lozen and the horse scrabbled down the steep bank and plunged into the water. And remember, she was on the horse with no stirrups or saddle to grab onto. She and the horse were soon across and scrambling up the other bank, out of range of the bullets.

Desert Crossing

Over the next few weeks Lozen, Eclode, and the baby endured harrowing adventures. Soldiers were guarding every water hole, so finding water was a big concern. Lozen collected a special cactus plant for them to chew, which offered some moisture.

As they traveled, Lozen continued to showcase her remarkable survival skills. She killed a calf for food and used its stomach as a water container. She stole a second horse from some vaqueros (Mexican cowboys). She ambushed another soldier and acquired more essential gear: a saddle, rifle, ammunition, and blanket, and an all-important canteen.

Many Names, Many People

Nowadays some Native American tribes that the US government officially recognizes have names that were given to them by others. "Apache" is one of those names. The origin of the name is widely debated. But it seems likely that it was given to them by their enemies. Spanish invaders may have created the word Apache as a way to label many different groups of Native people who lived in the southwestern part of what would eventually be the United States. Spanish colonists also named individual groups of Apache people according to where they encountered them. But Apache also means "enemy" in the language of a neighboring tribe called the Zuni. Several culturally related tribes are lumped under the Apache name, despite having their own unique histories. While some Apache people refer to themselves as Apache, others prefer to call themselves Dine'e, or Indé.

She even took his shirt—probably for herself to wear. After several weeks, the two managed to reach Eclode's people safely.

But it was there that Lozen learned about a terrible tragedy. Lozen's brother, Victorio, was dead.

Ambushed

The news finally reached the Mescalero Reservation. After Victorio and the rest of the group—about 160 in number—had left Lozen and Eclode, they'd camped in a desert region of Mexico in a place called Chihuahua. On the slopes of three rocky peaks, called Tres Castillos, they were ambushed by Mexican soldiers, and at least eighty Apache people were killed, including Victorio. About seventy more were taken prisoner. The captives were marched into the city of Chihuahua and sold into slavery.

Lozen was devastated by her brother's death and by what had happened to her people. She was probably haunted by the thought that had she been there, she might have been able to determine the enemy's whereabouts and helped the group evade the attack.

She immediately set off, traveling across the desert and avoiding US and Mexican patrols, to find those who had survived. She rejoined a group of people who had managed to get away, somewhere near the Sierra Madre, a mountain range in northern Mexico.

False Promises

Meanwhile, the Apache leader Geronimo and a different group of about 120 Apache rebels had also fled the reservation. Lozen and her group joined up with them. For several more years, they hid in the northern part of Mexico in the Sierra Madre,

eluding capture and carrying out raids on Mexican settlements.

By 1886 Geronimo and Lozen's small group of Apaches was pursued by five thousand US soldiers—*a quarter of the entire US army*—and as many as three thousand Mexican troops. But eventually Geronimo made a decision. The group had grown tired of running. They missed their families. So he sent Lozen and another woman, named Dahteste, to negotiate a truce.

It was then that they learned that another group of Apache people had been rounded up and sent to Florida by train. Realizing there was no other way to reunite with their families, Lozen and Geronimo's group agreed to surrender.

The US army general promised that after serving two years of prison in the East, Geronimo and his people would all be freed and would be permitted to return with their families to the reservation known as Turkey Creek in Arizona.

Not at Liberty

Lozen, Geronimo, and the rest of their group were put in chains and sent by train to captivity in Florida as political prisoners.

Once in Florida, the Apache people suffered in the humid climate and dismal living conditions. Many fell ill and died

Fugitives from Injustice

Three decades before Lozen and Eclode's harrowing journey, the United States had acquired a big chunk of land from Mexico after a war, in what is now known as the southwestern United States. The US government sent American soldiers to the area with orders to force all the Native people onto reservations.

By 1874 about four thousand Apache people, including Lozen and her brother, had been driven off their homelands and onto the San Carlos Reservation, in Arizona. The living conditions there were wretched. The barren land had no grass for horses and no game for hunting. Water was scarce. There were swarms of mosquitoes and venomous rattlesnakes. Starvation and disease killed many people.

Victorio, Lozen, and nearly three hundred Apache men, women, and children fled the reservation and returned to their homeland. For three years they evaded capture and clashed frequently with both US and Mexican cavalry (soldiers on horseback). Newspaper reporters described them with grudging admiration. Wrote one, "They knew the trails and passes and water holes of the vast mountain region in which they operated as well as a New Yorker knows the route between his house and his place of business." Wrote another, "They . . . make an average speed of eight miles an hour on foot, going in a kind of a jog trot, or in what soldiers would call 'double-quick' time." And another, "The mountain is their home and on

Two Apache men in a studio. Lozen may have worn similar clothing.

the mountain tops, eight or ten thousand feet above sea level, where every step makes a white man's heart beat like a trip hammer and his lungs nearly burst with the effort to breathe the Indian runs along with ease. . . . He can march on foot, in the roughest country, forty miles a day."

About the same time that Victorio and Lozen fled, other Apache leaders were captured, arrested, and brought to the reservation in chains. Among them was a Chiricahua Apache leader named Geronimo.

A young Jicarella Apache couple soon after their marriage.

of malaria, smallpox, and other diseases that their bodies had never encountered before. Some children were shipped off to government schools, where they were forced to cut their hair, wear European-style clothing, and speak only English.

After about a year of misery, some people were relocated to another fort in Alabama. Lozen was most likely part of that group. The government broke its promise to the Apache people and did not allow them to return to their land.

Geronimo, now old and still a prisoner of war, met with President Theodore Roosevelt in 1905. Geronimo pleaded with the president to honor the government's promise. The president refused. Despite pressure by people who were appalled by the government's policies,

the Apache prisoners would not be freed until 1913, four years after Geronimo died.

Eventually what was left of Lozen's group was permitted to relocate in the West again, on a reservation in Oklahoma. But Lozen was not among them. She had died during the long confinement, probably of tuberculosis. Although she never married and had no children of her own, her nephew—one of Victorio's sons—carried on the family line and helped keep her story alive.

In spite of everything Apache people endured at the hands of the US government, they have survived. Today there are eight federally recognized Apache tribes living in the United States, and many Apache people still live in Mexico.

Vesta Tilley

1864–1952

A Perfect Gentleman

Vesta Tilley made audiences roar with laughter moments after she stepped on-stage, strutting and singing. She was always impeccably dressed in men's cloth-ing. She even wore men's underwear un-derneath. Vesta would have looked super odd if she had on *women's* underwear, which would have meant a tight-laced corset, butt padding, and lots of frills—not very manlike. This was the late nine-teenth century after all, and the figure of the ideal woman at the time was sup-posed to resemble an hourglass.

Vesta Tilley was a type of performer called a male impersonator, someone who dresses and behaves in a way that mimics a traditionally masculine role. (Men also sometimes perform as women.

Both kinds of entertainment are now known as drag.) Playing a variety of male characters, she sang, danced, and enter-tained adoring audiences all over the world. She didn't try to make her high soprano voice deeper when she sang, which probably made her performance all the funnier to audiences at the time. But what seems to have most charmed her audiences was her skill at "punching up"—poking fun at vain, fussily dressed men and at formal, upper-class British society. Even the people who *were* fussily dressed men or from formal, upper-class British society thought Vesta was funny.

But her biggest fans were working-class women. They knew that Vesta came from their background, which probably made them appreciate her spot-on impersonations all the more. She became the highest-earning woman in Britain during the 1880s.

Family Connections

Vesta Tilley was a stage name. Her real name was Matilda Alice Powles. She was born in Worcester, England, the second of thirteen children. After she became famous, she seldom talked about her siblings, but she did leave them a lot of money in her will.

Her family was poor. Her father worked at a variety of jobs, including as a comic actor, factory worker, and music-hall manager, and later as Vesta's manager. Her mother was a dressmaker by trade but probably spent most of her time caring for those thirteen children.

Vesta's Star Rises

Little Matilda and her father developed a special bond. He began taking her along to rehearsals at the theater he managed. She loved the stage from the get-go and quickly learned to imitate many of the performers. She was three when she sang her first song onstage, and she was an instant hit. From then on, she became a regular performer. She and her father toured towns and cities throughout England for at least six months a year. Her stage name was the Great Little Tilley.

One day Vesta's father found her trying on his top hat and suit. He recognized a good idea when he saw it and had a child-sized evening suit made for her, complete with white tie and tails. She performed her first male role when she was six. She pretended to be a famous male opera singer named Sims Reeves, singing many of the same songs he did. Audiences howled with laughter. By the time she was eight, she was performing exclusively in male dress. As she said later, "I felt that I could express myself better if I were dressed as a boy."

When she was about ten, she changed her stage name to Vesta Tilley. By the time she was eleven, she was earning enough money to support her whole family. By then her father had resigned from his job and had become her personal manager and songwriter.

As Vesta got older, she developed a cast of male characters that she played, including an Eton schoolboy, a judge, a clergyman, a soldier, and a street urchin. Her comedic timing and carefully thought-out costumes thrilled her audiences. She performed in the United States to sold-out crowds as well. She also performed in pantomime shows.

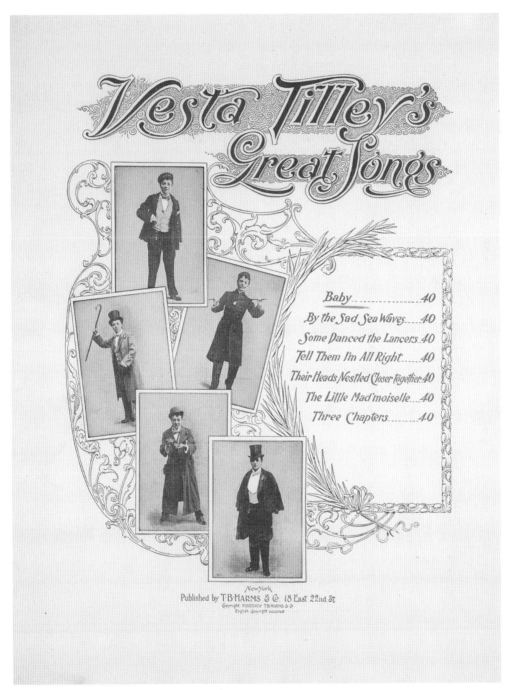

Vesta, dressed in some of her more popular outfits.

Vesta Performs in English Music Halls

Vesta came of age during a great period of music-hall theater in England, which spanned from about 1860 to 1920. In England, the birthplace of Shakespeare, theater was taken very seriously in this era. Literary dramatic productions were performed in only three London theaters. Anyone else who wanted to put on a performance had to do so in a music hall. They made sure that their show would not be confused with serious theater by adding something less serious—such as brass band or acrobats. Most music-hall theater consisted of a variety of acts that included popular songs, slapstick comedy, performing animals, acrobat tricks, and performances by male or female impersonators. Everyone knew the difference between high entertainment (real theater) and low entertainment (music-hall theater).

In the early days, music halls weren't considered appropriate places for respectable ladies or well-bred children. Female actors were usually thought to have questionable reputations. Sometimes male performers told off-color jokes and used vulgar language. Sometimes female performers wore risqué costumes, including trousers. Or sometimes women who danced revealed their legs from the

Note the "scandalous" display of women's legs in these advertisements.

Two Types of Entertainment

English Pantomime

When you see the word *pantomime*, you probably think about a mime, the type of performer who acts out a story without speaking, using only gestures and movements. But that's not what *pantomime* means in England. In Vesta's day, pantomime was a family-friendly musical comedy stage show, usually based on a well-known fairy tale or folktale, but full of slapstick comedy, silly jokes, and male characters played by women and female characters played by men. Early in Vesta's career, pantomime was considered the only respectable theater that women and children could attend.

Pantomime shows followed a general pattern. Usually the leading boy character was played by a woman. There was often an older woman character, who was usually played by a man. If there was an animal character, it was usually played by a human. The audience was encouraged to participate by shouting encouragement at performers or warning them of danger. *Peter Pan* comes from the pantomime tradition—the character of Peter is usually played by a woman, the dog is usually played by a human actor, and the audience is invited to shout helpful advice to assist the character Tinkerbell.

American Vaudeville

Over in the United States, theater was something of a free-for-all in the first part of the nineteenth century. Audiences let performers know what they thought of them by screaming, stamping their feet, throwing rotten fruit, or roaring for encores. After the Civil War, vaudeville promoters created a form of amusement that was a bit more restrained, geared toward the new class of better-off theatergoers who lived in larger towns and cities. Still, many vaudeville acts weren't very subtle. They included a lot of broad visual comedy and often offensive racial stereotypes.

On the stage, men have dressed in women's clothes since pre-Shakespearean days, and there were lots of men dressed as women in vaudeville. (One possible origin of the term "drag" to describe the art form comes from dragging one's petticoats on the ground.) But it was much rarer for a woman to be onstage dressed as a man, which is what made Vesta such a novelty. What we know today as "drag shows" began in the 1930s and may have originated in vaudeville.

knees down! Across the ocean in the United States, the equivalent to English music-hall entertainment was called vaudeville theater—also a series of separate, unrelated acts that appeared on one nightly program.

Gradually, by around 1880, both British music halls and American vaudeville theaters began offering more wholesome entertainment geared toward women and families. Producers realized that cleaning up the acts would result in a larger audience, which would mean more money from ticket sales.

Over the course of her career, Vesta helped change many people's opinion about musical theater. And also about women in trousers.

Loss and Love

Among Vesta's thousands of fans were many men who wanted to marry her, but her father strictly shielded her from suitors. Nevertheless, Vesta fell in love. His name was Walter de Frece. He was young, good-looking, and well-dressed— exactly the kind of character she played on the stage. Because he was the son of a music-hall developer and also Jewish, he was excluded from upper-crust British society. That might be one reason Vesta fell for him—because he was a bit of

an outsider like herself. Vesta's father approved of the young man, but they didn't marry right away. Perhaps Vesta's father discouraged the idea while Vesta's career was in full swing.

Vesta's father died suddenly from a fever (it may have been typhoid) in 1889. He was only forty-seven. After the sudden, devastating loss of her father, Vesta may have decided it was time to accept Walter's marriage proposal to fill the void that her father had left. A year later she and Walter were wed. It seems

Vesta in her later years.

to have been a strong and happy marriage. Walter built a successful business, creating a chain of musical-theater halls across England. Vesta kept performing.

The Height of Fame

It's challenging to reach back decades to try to capture what made a live performer seem so magical, charming, or humorous. There are recordings of Vesta's singing from the early twentieth century, but they don't show her acting or interacting with her audience, and that must have been a huge part of her appeal. But Vesta's performances delighted a wide range of people—men and women, children and adults—from every social class. She managed to poke fun at the male dominance of society by playing classic male roles—soldiers, sailors, and policemen. And she specialized in playing young aristocratic men in boaters and stiff collars or in tuxedoes, complete with a top hat, gloves, and cane.

Vesta's costumes imitated a perfectly dressed British man to an almost absurd degree, which British audiences found funny and which American audiences believed represented the height of sophistication and style. Offstage, Vesta made a point of dressing in the latest women's fashions. Possibly she did so to avoid

being criticized for her ever-more-daring onstage roles. She became a fashion icon.

Women loved Vesta because she was so good at mocking maleness. Working-class audiences loved her because she was so good at mocking the wealthy.

In 1920 Vesta retired from the stage. Her husband had been knighted in 1919 for his wartime work, and then he decided to run for public office. He became a member of Parliament. Vesta embraced a new role—she became Lady de Frece and spent the rest of her life in relative luxury. She died in 1952 at the age of eighty-eight.

Lilian Bland

1878–1971

That's a First

At the turn of the twentieth century, women who came from well-off, well-educated British or Irish families were expected to behave like ladies. They were supposed to take mincing, ladylike steps in their long, narrow skirts, find an eligible man to marry, and look forward to a life of embroidering sofa cushions. They were definitely *not* supposed to tinker with machines, toss on trousers, and jump behind the controls of a rickety aircraft.

Lilian Bland was not a typical ladylike lady, and *bland* is the last word you'd use to describe her. In 1910 she made history. She became the first person to fly a plane over Ireland. Risking life and limb, she managed to achieve liftoff with her heavier-than-air contraption, rising thirty feet off the ground. She flew about a quarter of a mile.

Also, because she flew in her *own* plane, she became the first woman *anywhere* to design, build, and fly her own motor-powered aircraft. She built it using bicycle handlebars, an empty whiskey bottle, and her aunt's ear trumpet.

An Era of Firsts

When Lilian built her plane, it was the dawn of the aviation era. People had been flying lighter-than-air aircraft, such as hot-air balloons, dirigibles, and blimps,

Lilian dressed and ready for action.

for decades already. But flying heavier-than-air machines with engines, wings, and rotors was something else entirely.

Seven years before Lilian's flight, back in 1903, Orville and Wilbur Wright were the first to fly a motorized air-craft—they did it on a beach at Kitty Hawk, North Carolina. Oddly the US government hadn't shown much interest in the Wright brothers' airplane. They were racking up lots of frequent-flyer miles, but the world did not become aware of what they accomplished until 1908, when the Wright brothers finally demonstrated their invention. They did it in France, flying their airplane

before a rapt crowd. *Now* people were paying attention. One year later a French aircraft designer named Louis Blériot became the first person to fly a plane from France to England.

The race was on. Early aviators competed to see who could be the first to build a better aircraft, and every-one scrambled to fly farther, faster, and higher. So Lilian's 1910 flight was very cutting edge.

Lilian's Wild Youth

Lilian was born in England to an Irish father and an English mother, youngest of three kids in a well-to-do family. When Lilian was in her early twenties, her mother died, and she moved with her father to a small village in Ireland to live with his widowed sister, Aunt Sarah.

The prim-and-proper neighbors were scandalized by Lilian. She gadded about in pants. She smoked cigarettes. She rode horses astride rather than sidesaddle. She hunted, fished, and fixed up cars. She was good at everything except acting like a lady.

Lilian took up her pen and wrote funny, engaging stories about sporting events. Her essays were published in London newspapers.

A year before she built her own plane, Lilian traveled with friends to Scotland, where she spent hours observing and photographing birds. She studied the curve of their wings, including the way birds maneuvered and tipped them to adjust altitude and direction. Her color photographs of birds in motion were published and praised. Perhaps it was all those long hours observing and studying birds' wing formations and flying patterns that led to her obsession with flight. It was from birds that she learned about angles and wind speeds and lift and drag.

While still in Scotland, she received a postcard from a relative. The card had a picture of Blériot's plane design, and it celebrated the Frenchman's famous flight across the English Channel. Lilian was hooked. She wrote to the great Blériot himself, asking if she could take a ride with him in his airplane. He responded with an emphatic "*non*." He didn't think women were suited for flying. Did that deter Lilian? Of course not. She decided to build her own plane.

The aptly named hobble skirt.

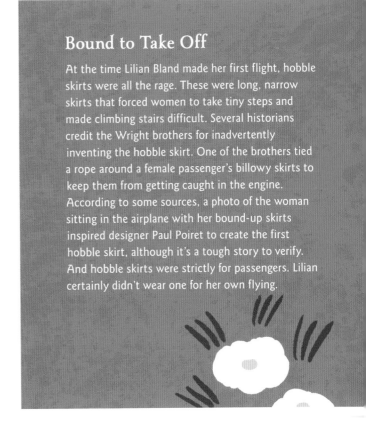

Bound to Take Off

At the time Lilian Bland made her first flight, hobble skirts were all the rage. These were long, narrow skirts that forced women to take tiny steps and made climbing stairs difficult. Several historians credit the Wright brothers for inadvertently inventing the hobble skirt. One of the brothers tied a rope around a female passenger's billowy skirts to keep them from getting caught in the engine. According to some sources, a photo of the woman sitting in the airplane with her bound-up skirts inspired designer Paul Poiret to create the first hobble skirt, although it's a tough story to verify. And hobble skirts were strictly for passengers. Lilian certainly didn't wear one for her own flying.

Lilian rode astride, although most women rode sidesaddle.

Mechanic

On her way home from Scotland, Lilian stopped off in England to attend an aviation conference. She joined several hundred thousand spectators who had come to watch and marvel at the new flying contraptions. She took careful notes, watched the way the planes flew, and then went home, determined to build Ireland's first heavier-than-air flying machine.

To fly in those early days was to risk your life: It was extremely difficult and extremely dangerous. Early airplanes

were made of wood, bamboo, wire, and fabric. Early aviators were half-fearless, half-wackadoo adventurers who braved bad weather, deafening noise, physical challenges, freezing temperatures, and the constant threat of injury and death. If they were lucky, pilots landed their plane and clambered out, half-frozen and spattered with motor oil. If they weren't, their machine upended or got caught in dangerous wind currents and crashed. Or their plane simply fell out of the sky.

In those days the only way to build a plane was to figure it out as you went. Lilian subscribed to a new magazine called *Flight*. She wrote about every stage of her project, and sent the articles to *Flight*, which published them.

Working in her deceased uncle's abandoned workshop, she built a model first. It had a six-foot wingspan and looked like a big airplane-shaped kite. Once she was satisfied with her design, she set out to build a full-size biplane, which is a plane with double wings. It began as a glider. That's an engineless plane that flies on wind currents—basically a bigger kite. Lilian's was made of ash, spruce, and elm wood, as well as paper and bamboo, and was held together with a series of struts and crisscrossing wires.

She modeled the construction of the wings after the curved wing tips of the birds she had photographed and studied. Her glider weighed about two hundred pounds and had a wingspan of a little over twenty feet. She named her flimsy contraption the *Mayfly*. As in, it may fly or it may not.

Pilot

Then Lilian had to teach herself how to fly. No flight schools existed. To learn, you simply had to . . . start flying. Some people survived. Some didn't.

She persuaded four burly Irish police constables, along with one of her aunt's gardeners, to help her test out her glider. They lugged her contraption up to the top of a nearby hill, and Lilian clambered into the pilot seat. Then she waited for the wind to lift the plane, while the men held tightly onto the ropes.

If the wind could lift the plane plus Lilian, she'd know that her glider would be able to handle the weight of an engine.

The wind lifted the plane. Plus Lilian. And also all four of the men. They managed to get the plane and themselves back down to earth safely.

Now it was time to add the engine.

So off Lilian went to England, where she bought a twenty-horsepower engine. Back in her workshop, she attached it to her plane with four bolts. She had ordered a fuel tank and tubing, but they hadn't yet arrived, so she improvised with an empty whiskey bottle for the tank and Aunt Sarah's ear trumpet for the fuel line. But when the engine's vibrations loosened the nuts and bolts, she decided to wait for the actual parts to show up.

A local wealthy landowner offered her the use of his fields as a place to test out the plane. But he warned her there was an angry bull on the property. Unperturbed, Lilian declared, "If it gets annoyed and charges I shall have every inducement to fly!"

Lilian's Model T would have looked much like this one.

Flight

In August 1910, with Lilian's gardener friend there to start the propeller, Lilian attempted her first flight. It was short and bumpy. She tinkered and adjusted stuff, and a few weeks later she tried again. This time the plane rose into the air and flew for about a quarter of a mile. She'd done it. She sent a write-up about her success to *Flight* magazine.

Do you think Lilian wore a skirt during all this? Of course not. Like all early aviators, she dressed to protect herself as best she could from cold, heat, sudden air blasts, noise, and oil splattering from the engine. "I find mechanic's overalls are the best things to wear," Lilian reported. "Skirts are out of the question with all the wires, etc., not to speak of oil."

Giddy with the success of her aircraft, Lilian decided to start her own company. She put an advertisement in the pages of *Flight* offering made-to-order gliders. This caused her family genuine alarm. The threat of calamity became real now that she'd proven that she knew how to get airborne. This "hobby" of hers was not just unladylike—it was downright dangerous. Her father offered to buy her a car—a brand-new Ford Model T— if she promised to abandon flying.

Motorist

Cars had been around for a few decades by that time, but it had only been about three years since the first Ford Model T had been produced in 1908. So her father's offer was super tempting to thrill-seeking Lilian. Early automobiles could go way faster than early airplanes. The Wright brothers' flights had traveled thirty miles per hour. A motorist in an automobile could travel as fast as seventy miles per hour. Lilian was running low on money, and she knew she'd need a lot more to fund a better aircraft. Also, she'd done what she'd set out to do. She'd become the first person to fly over Ireland. So she gave up flying and took up driving.

Her father's offer, motivated by a desire to keep his spirited daughter safe, seems somewhat ineffective if you think about it. Traveling by car in 1911 wasn't much safer than traveling by airplane. Roadways had no stop signs, no traffic lights, no streetlights, and no speed limits. There was no driver's education to learn to drive. Cars had no brake lights, seat belts, blinkers, or gas pedals. They were so top-heavy, they often turned over as they took corners—newspapers called that "turtling." Yet Lilian quickly figured out how to drive. This is not as easy as you might think.

Soon Lilian was a master driver. The Ford Motor Company hired her to be their chief sales agent in Belfast, Ireland.

Lilian never went back to flying, but she lived a long and exciting life none-theless. She married, moved to Canada, had a kid, divorced, and eventually settled down in a house in the English countryside. She lived to the ripe old age of ninety-two.

Frida Kahlo

1907–1954

She's the Man

An early photo of artist Frida Kahlo, taken by her father, shows a nineteen-year-old Frida wearing a three-piece men's suit and tie, her hair smoothed back like a debonair fellow. A later photo shows Frida wearing cuffed jeans and smoking a cigarette. In a 1941 painting called *Self-Portrait with Cropped Hair*, Frida depicts herself in a baggy men's suit, her hair in a manly bob. In numerous self-portraits, she carefully paints her own dark facial hair—a unibrow and mustache, intentionally calling attention to her masculine side.

Frida Kahlo was always comfortable with cross-dressing, no matter what the current fashions were. Nowadays we might describe her as gender fluid, someone who doesn't identify as having a fixed gender that is the same all the time. But in her day, that language did not yet exist. She was simply seen as fiercely independent. The fame she achieved during her lifetime was sometimes attributed to her being the wife of a more famous artist. And yet history has proven otherwise.

The Accident

It was a late September afternoon in 1925. Eighteen-year-old Frida Kahlo was riding a wooden bus through the streets of Mexico City when a trolley car plowed into it. In a sort of grotesque slow motion, the trolley pushed the bus across the road. Then the bus splintered into pieces.

Frida lay in the street. An iron handrail had been driven clear through her abdomen. Her spine and pelvis were broken in three places. Her right leg was broken in eleven places. Her right foot was dislocated and crushed. Her left shoulder was out of joint, and her collarbone and three ribs were broken.

It's a wonder she survived. But survive she did, although she endured a month in the hospital and operation after operation. She spent most of the next year at home in bed in a series of full-body casts. She needed a way to pass the time. Her father brought her paints. Her mother put a mirror on the canopy above her bed, so she could see her own reflection. Frida painted with growing enthusiasm.

She did her first self-portrait at age nineteen, while she was still recovering from her injuries. She soon abandoned her dream of becoming a doctor. She would be a painter instead. There were few, if any, famous women painters to serve as role models. But Frida had never been a conventional sort of girl. Most of her friends at school were boys. She cut her hair short and liked to wear blue overalls. So her atypical career choice was consistent with her rebellious personality.

As she told her mother, "I'm still alive and besides, I have something to live for, and that something is painting."

Frida's Early Years

Frida's real name was Magdalena Carmen Frieda Kahlo Calderón, but as a child everyone called her Frieda. (She eventually dropped the *e* from "Frieda.") Her family lived in a bright-blue house at the outskirts of Mexico City. Her father, Guillermo Kahlo, was a Hungarian German Jewish photographer. Her mother, Matilde Calderón, was mestiza, of mixed Indigenous (native Mexican) and Spanish ancestry.

Frida was the third of four girls. Her early childhood was a happy one, although beyond the walls of Frida's blue house, there was lots of political upheaval in Mexico. When Frida was three, the Mexican Revolution began. The violence and armed conflicts dragged on for ten years and resulted in radical changes in the government.

When Frida was six, she felt a terrible pain in her leg. She'd contracted a spinal disease—possibly polio.

Frida survived the disease, but her right leg would always be shorter than her left, and she limped for the rest of her life. As a kid she often wore boys' clothing—wearing pants helped hide the difference in her legs' lengths, but

Frida as a young girl.

she also showed an early interest in presenting a unique image of herself to the world.

Frida attended a highly regarded high school in Mexico City called Escuela Nacional Preparatoria. She was one of only thirty-five girls in a school of two thousand. She was an excellent student.

For centuries Mexican history had been taught from a European point of view. But when the revolution finally ended, the country underwent a cultural and artistic renaissance. Mexican people showed a newfound pride in their country's past, especially the time before the Spanish conquistadors arrived. The Mexican government hired artists to paint murals on public buildings with scenes that celebrated the country's history and that helped create a new sense of Mexican national identity.

In 1922 one of these artists came to Frida's school to paint a mural in the auditorium. His name was Diego Rivera. He was already quite famous, and Frida was fascinated by him. Students had been warned not to disturb the great artist. But ever the rule breaker, Frida sometimes crept into the auditorium and observed him as he worked.

Frida and Diego

A few years later, Frida crossed paths with Diego Rivera again at a party. She was twenty-one. He was forty-one. She was five foot three and weighed less than a hundred pounds. He was over six feet tall and weighed more than three hundred pounds. The physically mismatched couple fell in love. In 1929 they were married.

Frida's father approved of the marriage. Certain that Frida would have health problems for the rest of her life, he wanted his daughter to be with a man who could earn enough money to take care of her. Frida's mother did not approve. Frida was Diego's third wife. He'd been divorced twice. He was known to have had affairs with many women. Also, Diego was old and overweight.

Frida's mother likened their marriage to one between an elephant and a dove.

By the time they'd been married for a year, Diego had become internationally famous. He was invited to travel to the United States to paint several murals. The couple moved first to San Francisco, then to New York, and then to Detroit.

Few people knew that Frida was also an artist. In 1933 only one of the local writers assigned to cover Diego's visit paid any attention to Frida—and that was the sole female reporter in the group. She wrote an article about Frida. But the headline the newspaper ran for Frida's interview read "Wife of the Master Mural Painter Gleefully Dabbles in Works of Art." Still, Frida got a chance to show her fiery independent side. "Of course he

[Diego] does pretty well for a little boy," she says in the article, "but it is I who am the big artist."

She Blended Her Art with Her Life

During their three years in the United States, Frida continued to paint. She became pregnant but had a miscarriage at three months. Although she wanted a child, she was never physically well enough to bear one. She expressed her pain and sadness through her paintings.

She made mostly self-portraits and still lifes. In several paintings of fruits and flowers, she wrote *Viva la Vida* (which loosely translates to "Live your life"). But Frida's life was largely lived through her art. In art, Frida believed, beautiful things stayed beautiful forever. In real life, they were doomed to rot or decay.

At first her work was mostly ignored. At fancy events that she and Diego attended, she continued to be introduced merely as Diego's wife. But soon people began to take notice of Frida's work.

The subject of Frida's paintings was often herself, and her personal style evolved and changed. Sometimes she wore pants. Other times she showed pride in her Mexican heritage by wearing long, flowing, brightly colored dresses and masses of necklaces, rings, and

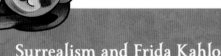

Surrealism and Frida Kahlo

Whether she liked it or not, Frida Kahlo is now considered one of the world's greatest surrealists. Surrealism was an artistic movement that was often identified with dreamlike scenes and the workings of the unconscious mind. The most famous surrealist is Salvador Dalí—maybe you've seen his painting of melting clocks.

"They thought I was a Surrealist but I wasn't," Frida told a reporter. "I never painted dreams. I painted my own reality."

The side-by-side homes of Frida and Diego with a walkway between them.

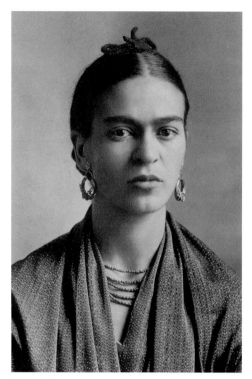

Frida Kahlo.

shawls. She braided and then piled her long hair on top of her head and festooned it with flowers.

Together, Apart, and Together Again

Frida and Diego returned to Mexico. Their relationship had been a stormy one from the beginning, and it continued to be. Both had affairs with other people—in Frida's case, with women as well as with men. For a time they lived together in a house with two wings—one side was Frida's, the other Diego's—connected on the second floor by a footbridge. That seemed to work pretty well for a time.

But then Frida discovered that Diego was having an affair with her younger sister, Cristina. In her anguish at being betrayed by the two people she loved most, Frida cut off her long hair and stopped painting. The couple separated in 1935. They would continue to quarrel, get back together, and quarrel again for many more years. They seemed to be unable to live with each other for long but grew deeply unhappy when they lived apart. In 1939 they finally got a divorce.

A year later they remarried each other. Frida later wrote, "There have been two great accidents in my life. One was the trolley, and the other was Diego. Diego was by far the worst."

Frida's Fame Grows

In 1938 Frida had her first solo exhibition, held in New York City. A year later the Louvre, in Paris, bought one of her paintings. Style-conscious women began imitating her fashion. French *Vogue* put her on the cover.

Frida's reputation as an artist began to soar. But as her fame grew, Frida's health worsened. Eventually her spine became so weak that she could not sit or stand without support. Doctors fitted her for a series of different plaster, leather, and metal corsets.

She took up teaching and had a devoted following of students. She had inherited the bright-blue house after her parents died, and she lived there happily, sometimes with Diego, sometimes not. In the lush garden she kept dogs, cats, deer, doves, ducks, parrots, and monkeys, many of which appear in her paintings.

Frida learned with delight that she was to have her first-ever exhibition in Mexico in 1953. But she'd endured a series of operations on her spine that had left her weaker and even more gravely ill. On the day of the opening, her doctors told her she should not leave her bed. Frida refused to stay home. She arranged to have her bed loaded into the back of a truck, driven to the exhibition opening, and set up in the center of the gallery. Minutes before the party began, Frida arrived in an ambulance accompanied by a motorcycle escort. She was carried inside on a stretcher and placed on her bed, where she greeted guests all evening. In characteristic fashion, Frida's real-life self became part of her own exhibition.

Less than a year later, she died in the same blue house in which she'd been born. She was only forty-seven years old.

Her Parting Gift

Frida's work was largely overshadowed during her lifetime by her larger-than-life husband. Her obituary headline in the *New York Times* read "Frida Kahlo, Artist, Diego Rivera's Wife." But nowadays many art experts believe that she was a better artist than Diego.

Her last painting was a still life of lush red watermelons. Eight days before she died, she signed her name to it and added her famous words *Viva la Vida*.

Diego donated Frida's blue house to the Mexican government. Today it is the Frida Kahlo Museum.

Diego died three years after Frida did. His final painting was also a still life of watermelons.

Marcenia "Toni" Stone

1921–1996

The New Recruit

Marcenia Lyle Stone was twelve years old when her parents met with their local priest, Father Charles Keefe. Marcenia's parents begged him to talk their daughter out of playing baseball. They thought it was unladylike for a girl to play with the neighborhood boys. They thought it was inappropriate for her to dress like a boy to play baseball. They wanted her to grow up and get a good job. Playing baseball was not what they considered a good job.

Father Keefe agreed to do what he could and arranged a meeting with Marcenia. She confessed to Father Keefe that if her parents refused to let her play, she had no choice but to run away. She couldn't give up baseball.

Father Keefe was well respected by people in the neighborhood. The priest knew Marcenia and her family. He knew that her nickname was Tomboy Stone. He knew that she was a phenomenal athlete. She was good at every sport she tried—swimming, golf, track, basketball, hockey, tennis, and skating—but she lived and breathed baseball.

As it turned out, Father Keefe didn't push her to quit baseball. Instead he offered her a spot on the church's team. As luck would have it, he was the coach.

Somehow Father Keefe convinced Marcenia's parents that letting her play was a good idea. It *was* a church team, after all. And she was good. She became a sensation in Saint Paul, Minnesota, playing first for Father Keefe's church team and later for other boys' teams in the city.

The 1920s and 1930s were the golden age of Negro league baseball. Young Marcenia, who was Black, idolized all the greats, like Satchel Paige, James "Cool Papa" Bell, and Josh Gibson. She studied the rule book. She pored over the sports pages. She learned the game inside and out. The Negro leagues were the Black players' equivalent of the all-white major leagues. Negro league teams rented space in vacant stadiums to play games when white major league teams were away.

Thousands of fans, white as well as Black, flocked to Negro league games. Whatever their view was on the subject of racial equality, fans wanted to see great baseball. Although Black players often faced discrimination, disrespect, and even violence off the field, they were able to show white spectators that Black players were among the best in the game.

Marcenia's mom, still holding out hope that her daughter might be persuaded to give up baseball for a more feminine sport, bought her daughter some figure skates. Marcenia entered a citywide figure skating competition and won a first-place trophy. "I took it home, and gave it to my mother, and picked up my glove and bat. She knew then that I wasn't going to give up baseball."

If You Give a Girl a Throwing Arm . . . She's Going to Want to Play Baseball

Marcenia's parents—who seem to have finally thrown in the towel—let fifteen-year-old Marcenia join a barnstorming team. Barnstormers traveled from town to town, playing nonleague exhibition games against both Black and white semipro teams. Crowds paid. Marcenia was the only girl on her team. She wore the same billowy-trousered uniform as her teammates. She played infield, outfield, and occasionally pitcher.

The Black barnstorming teams were poorly paid and haphazardly organized. But the one goal practically every player had in common was to make it to the Negro leagues.

The War Years

Marcenia headed to San Francisco in 1943 to live with her sister, Bunny, and her sister's husband. She had no money and no job. But San Francisco offered better employment opportunities for Black people. She soon found work at the shipyards, driving trucks. She wore men's work shirts and pants.

By this point Marcenia had changed her name to Toni. Maybe she was tired

Toni Stone, pro-baller.

of her nickname Tomboy, or maybe she thought Toni sounded more like a baller than Marcenia. One day Toni met the owner of a men's semipro barnstorming team called the San Francisco Sea Lions. He invited her to join the team. At her first at-bat, she drove in two runs.

Toni endured hostility from both her male opponents and her own teammates. When she played second base, runners slid into the base with their spikes up. Her own teammates took their time scooping up ground balls and then lobbed them to her, thus setting her up for a collision with the base runner. But she put up with it because she loved the game. And management loved her, because her presence on the team helped sell a lot of tickets.

When she discovered she was earning less than her male teammates, she left the team. She eventually joined the New Orleans Creoles, another minor league team. Crowds came to see her make great plays in the outfield and bat .265. Her fame was spreading.

The Big Time

By 1950 Toni's name had national recognition. After the season ended, she surprised everyone by getting married to a much older man, whom she'd met in San Francisco. It seemed to be a happy marriage.

Meanwhile one of the Negro league teams—the Indianapolis Clowns—had just lost their star infielder. His name was Hank Aaron. He'd been called into the major leagues, which were slowly opening their doors to Black players.

So the next season, the owner of the Indianapolis Clowns signed Toni. She played second base, the position Hank Aaron had vacated. Listed at twenty-two years old, she was actually thirty-two.

The team owner dared to suggest to Toni that she wear a short skirt and satin shorts combo to play, just as the women in the all-white girls' baseball league did. Toni flatly refused. She would wear her team's uniform. When Toni stepped onto the field in her Clowns uniform, she became the first woman ever to play professional major-league baseball.

Playing in the Negro leagues must have been both thrilling and dispiriting for Toni. She drew big crowds full of curious people who wanted to see a woman play. But if Black male players faced difficulties, consider how hard it was to be the only Black female player.

When the team traveled to still-segregated southern states, Toni's team struggled to find hotels and restaurants that would serve them. As a Black

Satchel Paige.

woman, Toni often faced twice the discrimination.

Toni played one more season, this time with the Kansas City Monarchs, before she retired to care for her aging husband. She continued to coach and play semipro ball well into her sixties. She enjoyed showing off the scars on her wrist where long ago she'd been spiked by a runner trying to slide into her as she blocked second base. "He was out," she said.

Best Day Ever

Long after she had retired, Toni was asked by a reporter if she could recall the happiest day of her life. She answered right away.

It was Easter Sunday in 1953. The great pitcher Satchel Paige, whom Toni had idolized as a girl, had agreed to play an exhibition game against the Clowns—Toni's team. He liked to give the crowd its money's worth, and in typical showboat fashion, he asked each batter what kind of pitch he wanted. Fast? Slow? Straight up the middle?

It didn't matter. One after another, Paige struck them all out.

Then Toni stepped up to the plate.

"Hey, T!" shouted Satchel. "How do you like it?"

Toni was a bundle of nerves. "It doesn't matter," she croaked. "Just don't hurt me."

Paige went into his windup and fired a fastball over the plate. She laced it over the second baseman's head into center field. It was a base hit—the only hit of the day. She laughed giddily as she ran to first. When she turned, Satchel was laughing too.

Years later, she smiled as she recollected that hit. "It was a lulu," she said.

Batter up!

Girls Playing Ball

Evening the Score

Baseball is America's national pastime. So why is it that half the population doesn't get to play?

Because *softball* is for girls, right? Well, no. Softball was invented in 1887 as a game for men. Softball is a great sport, but it is not the same as baseball. Girls started playing softball only when they got shut out of baseball.

In baseball's early days, both boys and girls played the game in schoolyards. In the 1870s several women's colleges formed teams, but for white women only.

Around the same time, the first semipro women's baseball teams (all white) were formed by businessmen who hoped to attract paying crowds. But it wasn't serious baseball. Team owners told players to put on a show to boost ticket sales. Players caught balls in their skirts and clowned around at the plate.

Little League baseball began in 1939. For boys only.

During the Second World War, many male ballplayers left to fight overseas. So promoters created the All-American Girls Professional Baseball League (AAGPBL) in 1943. Once again, only white women could play. Teams were given girly-girl names like the Milwaukee Chicks, the Fort Wayne Daisies, and the Rockford Peaches.

In 1973, after multiple court battles, Little League officials reluctantly allowed girls to play.

In 2014 thirteen-year-old Mo'ne Davis became the first girl to pitch a shutout and earn a win in the Little League World Series.

And in 2015 the US Women's National Baseball Team won a gold medal at the Pan-American Games in Toronto, Canada. It was the first international sporting event to feature women's baseball.

Silly Stuff They Wore

Female college baseball players in the 1870s played in full-length skirts, long-sleeve shirts, and high-button shoes. When a batter hit the ball, she dropped the bat, hiked up her skirts, and ran to first base.

By the 1880s, some women's college teams began wearing bloomers. Games were played in private areas where there were no gawking men around.

During the 1890s for the brief period when women played serious professional baseball, the players wore billowy pants and were known as Bloomer Girls. Only white women were allowed.

In the All-American Girls Professional Baseball League of the 1940s, players wore short, flared skirts with satin shorts underneath. They attended charm school and reviewed how to walk properly, apply makeup, and talk with the press. Players were required to wear lipstick at all times.

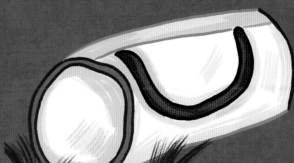

Marguerite Johnson

1928–2014

Unsuitable

In the early 1940s, a teenage girl named Marguerite Johnson arrived at the offices of the Market Street Railway Company in San Francisco, California. She had come to apply for a job. World War II was raging. With so many American men away fighting, the US government had begun a campaign to encourage American women to join the labor force. More and more women were finding jobs outside the home. But it was a deeply racist time. The best jobs were reserved for white women. Marguerite was Black.

At the railway company, the clerk turned Marguerite away before she could even fill out an application. The job was only for white women. But as history would soon prove, this was a girl with gumption.

Marguerite was born in Saint Louis, Missouri, in 1928. She and her younger brother lived with their grandmother in Arkansas but later rejoined their mother, Vivian, in San Francisco. Marguerite was still in high school, but by the time she got to San Francisco, it was too late to enroll in school for the fall. Because Marguerite was ahead in her schooling, her mother suggested she get a job for a semester. Poring over the help-wanted listings in the newspaper, Marguerite lasered in on the ad for female cable-car conductors. She'd noticed white women conductors on the job, and their snazzy uniforms—complete with pants—thrilled her. "I saw women on the streetcars with their little changer belts. . . . And they had caps with bills on them and they had form-fitting jackets," she later recalled. A cable-car conductor—that was the job she wanted.

So when the clerk sent her away, her hopes were dashed. But not for very long.

Factory Fashion

Around the time Marguerite was turned away for the cable-car conductor job, a song called "Rosie the Riveter" hit the airwaves. It was wildly popular. Working women now had a name—Rosie—and having a job outside the home became their patriotic duty. More than six million American women answered the call for recruitment. They worked in shipyards, lumber mills, steel mills, and defense plants. They trained as electricians and mechanics. They operated streetcars, buses, cranes, and tractors. And huge numbers stepped out of their skirts and put on pants, coveralls, and masculine-looking uniforms to do the work.

With very few exceptions, the posters, advertisements, and newsreels depicted only white women. Contributions by women of color were rarely recorded. In fact there were thousands of Black and Brown Rosie the Riveters.

Determined

When Marguerite Johnson got home the day she was turned away, she told her mother what the clerk had said. Her mother told her to go back to the office and ask again.

And so she did. And her gumption paid off.

"I sat [there] for two weeks, every day," she recalled later. "And then after two weeks, a man came out of his office and said, 'Come here.' And he asked me, 'Why do you want the job?' I said, 'I like the uniforms.' And I said, 'And I like people.' And so I got the job."

And with that, Marguerite became the first-ever Black streetcar conductor—man or woman—in San Francisco. Marguerite's stubbornness and perseverance, plus a healthy fear of her mom's displeasure, helped her make history.

Super Conductor

If landing the job was the only big thing Marguerite ever did, she'd still have secured a spot in the history books. But that turned out to be the *least* of her accomplishments. She grew to a ravishing six-foot height. She became a singer and a dancer. And then a poet and a writer. She wrote seven autobiographies, three books of essays, several books of

Rosie the Riveter: World War II symbol of patriotic womanhood.

A Symbol of Patriotism

Ever hear of Rosie the Riveter? Maybe you've seen her picture. Back in the 1940s, the American government produced films and ads showing cheerful women hard at work hammering, welding, and even, yes, riveting, which, as everyone knows, means fastening metal doohickeys together with a thingamabob.

But there was no real person named Rosie the Riveter. She was a symbol, an idealized image of a patriotic woman. Those posters and newsreels showing her hard at work were part of an ad campaign to get American women fired up to do their patriotic duty—filling jobs vacated by men.

Today the most famous picture of Rosie is the one shown here. But it wasn't famous during the war years. It was produced by an artist hired by a company that manufactured equipment for the war and was displayed only internally as a way to motivate workers. The most famous Rosie picture during the war was painted by the artist Norman Rockwell.

poetry, and two cookbooks. She became an actor, playwright, director, and producer of numerous plays, movies, and television shows. She worked as a civil rights activist alongside both Martin Luther King Jr. and Malcolm X. Later in life she was a professor of American studies. In 1993 she wrote and recited a poem at the inauguration of President Bill Clinton. She raised a son who grew up to be a poet himself, and she had several husbands. After divorcing one of them, she blended her childhood nickname with a shortened version of that husband's last name and used it as her professional name.

Marguerite Johnson, the first Black streetcar conductor in San Francisco, grew up to become Maya Angelou. Now *that's* a name that might ring a bell.

From a Hard Life to a Starred Life

Marguerite had not had an easy childhood. But when she was a teenager, she

Still Deeply Divided

Finding decent paid employment had never been easy for Black women. As Marguerite Johnson discovered, that continued even during the war, when more and more jobs were available. When white women went to work in factories and for the government, Black women filled the sudden demand for domestic workers. They were hired by white women to perform the tasks that the white women had abandoned—caring for children and doing the housework. It was work, but domestic jobs did not pay as well as government and factory jobs.

As the war dragged on, manufacturers needed more and more workers. But many American workplaces were still racially segregated. In 1943 twenty-two white women walked out of a Western Electric plant in Baltimore, Maryland, to protest the fact that Black women had been hired in their department. But eventually, in the later years of the war, some Black women were able to leave low-paid domestic work and find decent-paying jobs.

Black women World War II workers, overlooked by many historians.

received a scholarship to study dance. She worked as a streetcar conductor during the six months before she started dance school.

By the time Maya reached her twenties, she was an accomplished singer, dancer, and actor. She toured with a production of the opera *Porgy and Bess* alongside world-famous singers. They performed in twenty-two countries. She met famous writers such as Langston Hughes and John Oliver Killens. It was Killens who convinced her to move to New York permanently and to consider a writing career.

Maya joined the Harlem Writers Guild, where she met the author James Baldwin. In 1968, he took her to a dinner party at the home of the famous cartoonist Jules Feiffer. Maya so charmed the guests with stories about her life that the next day, Feiffer's wife called an editor at Random House and suggested he get Maya to write a memoir. The editor called Maya and pitched the idea.

"Absolutely not," said Maya.

The next time he called, he slyly remarked that it was just as well she didn't want to, "because to write an autobiography as literature is just about impossible."

That worked. Maya loved a challenge.

"I said, 'I'll start tomorrow,'" Maya remembered. She proceeded to write *I Know Why the Caged Bird Sings*. The book made literary history as the first nonfiction bestseller by an African American woman.

Maya went on to receive a Tony Award nomination for her role in a play called *Look Away* and an Emmy Award nomination for her work on a TV miniseries called *Roots*.

In 2011 President Barack Obama presented her with the Presidential Medal of Freedom. That's the highest honor a civilian can receive.

Maya died at age eighty-six. In his tribute, President Obama quoted the title of Maya's own poem "Phenomenal Woman" when he called her "a brilliant writer, a fierce friend, and a truly phenomenal woman."

AUTHOR'S NOTE

My Checkered Past

When I was in third grade, I showed up at school wearing a black-and-white checked pantsuit. It was the seventies, so I'm pretty sure it was a hundred percent polyester. I thought I looked extremely "dy-no-mite." My class was going on a field trip—some sort of outdoor nature expedition—and I figured that surely the dress code for girls wouldn't apply that day.

I was wrong.

The school principal called my parents. My dad had to leave work and bring me a skirt to change into.

That was a pivotal moment in my life—an awakening of sorts. I became suddenly aware that double standards and dumb rules existed, and a lot of them were unfair to girls in particular.

The following year, my fourth-grade gym teacher divided our class into groups: boys and girls. When I learned that the boys would head off to the other side of the divider to play basketball while the girls learned "dance," I put my tiny foot down. (I was the smallest kid in my class.) *I* wanted to play basketball.

I was ordered to sit on the sidelines. As punishment, I couldn't participate in either activity.

These episodes caused me to develop a strong sense of indignation. I became keenly aware of injustice and was quick to point it out. I was a really fun little sister, as I bet you can tell. Just ask my older siblings.

If You Give a Girl a Basketball . . .

Back in the day, girls like me were called tomboys. Nowadays many such girls are known as good athletes. I grew up (and up some more) and became a college basketball player. Luckily I came of age at a time when attitudes about what girls should wear and what sports they should play were changing. Still, my early experiences stayed with me. Those feelings of indignation were knitted into the fabric of my personality. Maybe that's why I wrote this book. Maybe the cumulative impact of those feelings prompted me to seek out bigger stories of injustice and triumph.

It's taken a few centuries, but at long last women can dress more or less as they please in many (but by no means all) parts of the world. In this book, you've seen how far we've come since the days when most women were not free to travel without a male escort, to rule, to earn their own money, to fight for their country, or to pursue a chosen profession.

We've come a long way, but there's still a lot further to go before women run an equal share of all countries, companies, armies, universities, sports teams, and movie studios.

You can help the world keep evolving.

Athletics: Not a Good Idea for Girls

Enslaved women, frontier women, and female farmers and servants have engaged in strenuous activity for centuries without anyone getting too frothed up about what overexertion might do to their health and well-being. But ever since ancient Athens, when athletics were a naked-male-only pastime, sports and exercise for upper-class women—from riding horses astride to brisk walks to a vigorous game of croquet—tended to be frowned upon in much of the Western world. Books such as one published in 1827 called *A Treatise on Calisthenic Exercises: Arranged for the Private Tuition of Ladies* suggested that mild calisthenics could be beneficial for women, so long as they weren't too strenuous. And when basketball was introduced in the 1890s, special rules were created for girls. They had to stick to confined zones, lest they overexert themselves or dislodge their uterus.

A strenuous workout for delicate ladies.

Acknowledgments

I am grateful to many people for their support, advice, and guidance with this book. Thanks to specialists and expert readers Renee S. Bear Medicine, Blackfeet anthropologist, Museum of the Plains Indian; Dr. Pavel Rykin, senior research fellow, Institute for Linguistic Studies, Russian Academy of Sciences; Dr. Sara Hume, associate professor and curator, Kent State University Museum; Jean Druesedow, museum director, Kent State University Museum; Dr. Enrique R. Lamadrid, distinguished professor emeritus of Spanish and Portuguese, University of New Mexico; Robert Martinez, New Mexico deputy state historian; Dr. Lucianne Lavin, director of research and collections, Institute for American Indian Studies Museum; Mark Mennin, sculptor and art historian; Andrew Prince, history teacher and dean of multicultural education, the Taft School; Kieran Slattery, MA children's literature, Simmons University; and Mercedes Acosta, children's author/ illustrator and Taíno storyteller. Any errors are mine and not those of any of my expert readers.

Thanks as well to my writer friends and readers for reviewing the manuscript at multiple stages: Loree Griffin Burns, Melissa Stewart, April Jones Prince, Kate Narita, Kathryn Hulick, Michaela Muntean, Marcia DeSanctis, Cassie Willson, Jon Willson, Gina Drayton Ludlow, Traci Sorell, and Nandini Bajpai. Thanks to my sister, Marina Albee, for her ongoing support and help putting me in touch with experts across the world.

Thanks to all the librarians at the Taft School for helping me dig up facts and primary sources that I never would have found otherwise, for tracking down articles in obscure academic journals, and for my dozens of interlibrary loan requests, with special amens to Patti Taylor, Sean Padgett, Beth Lovallo, Betsy Barber, and Janet Kenney. Thanks as well to the many, many reference librarians—nonfiction writers' best friends—for their assistance, particularly those at Darien Public Library, Wesleyan University Library, Widener Library at Harvard University, the Library of Congress, and my home-away-from-home, the New York Public Library, with a special shout to the librarians in the rare book division.

Ongoing thanks to all my Nerdy Book Club teacher and librarian friends for their infectious and boundless love for reading and for putting books by authors and illustrators into the hands of their students. We couldn't do this without you.

Thanks to my wonderful agent Caryn Wiseman and to the amazing team at Charlesbridge, including designer Jon Simeon for his gorgeous book design. Thanks to copyeditor Hannah Mahoney and proofreader Jackie Dever—their stupendous work and fact-checking skills saved me more than a few times. And a special thanks to illustrator Kaja Kajfež for her breathtaking illustrations.

There aren't enough superlatives to describe my wondrous editor, Karen Boss. I won't attempt to try because she'd probably make me take out all the adjectives anyway, along with two-thirds of my commas. I'm proud of this book, and it would never have been possible without her vision, guidance, and wisdom. She's the man.

Notes

Please see the bibliography on pages 155–159 for more information about the cited works.

Introduction: Suit Yourself

p. viii: "The generally accepted rule . . . prettier for the girl": *Earnshaw's Infants' Departments*, June 1918, quoted in Maglaty.

p. ix: In the 1960s . . . tunic top: Zinko.

p. ix: In 2016 . . . instead of a dress: Flam.

p. ix: As recently as 2016 . . . rookie-orientation program: Cretaz.

King of Queens: Hatshepsut

p. 1: To give you an idea . . . years old: Roehrig, Dreyfus, and Keller, p. 3.

p. 2: Pictures from this time . . . leadership role: Roth, p. 9.

p. 3: [sidebar] Hatshepsut became close . . . definitely in charge: Keller, pp. 295–96.

p. 7: People now believe . . . remains of Hatshepsut: Wilford.

p. 7: Or possibly she died . . . skin condition: Cohen.

Amazon Prime: Hypsicratea

p. 10: "a girl always . . . Persian horseman": Clough, p. 91.

p. 10: Mithradates's soldiers . . . rotating blades: Mayor, *Poison King*, p. 149.

p. 11: Hypsicratea fought . . . king's castles: Mayor, *Poison King*, pp. 320–23.

p. 11: At first Pompey . . . Amazon warriors: Mayor, *Poison King*, p. 328, 331; Mayor, *Amazons*, p. 345.

p. 11: [sidebar] "arrange your skirts under your butt.": Mayor, Amazons, p. 195.

p. 12: [sidebar] Here's what ancient . . . probably true): Worrall.

p. 13: Here's one . . . Amazon queen?: Mayor, *Amazons*, pp. 350–51.

p. 13: In 2010 Russian . . . has been lost: Mayor, *Poison King*, p. 356; Mayor, *Amazons*, p. 351.

Vested Interest: Khutulun

p. 15: It might have looked . . . between wars: Krippes, p. 99.

p. 15: The uniform design . . . title still stands: Weatherford, "Wrestler"; Weatherford, *Secret*, p. 274.

p. 16: To cement his power . . . fight in his army: Weatherford, *Secret*, p. 30.

p. 16: She rode at his side . . . thousands of warriors: Mayor, *Amazons*, p. 402.

p. 17: Like the Scythians . . . effective as a man: Weatherford, *Secret*, pp. 120–21.

p. 17: The silk wouldn't tear . . . arrow out: Davison, p. 172.

p. 18: "young and handsome . . . in every way": Yule, p. 394.

p. 18: "gladly be his wife . . . not otherwise": Ibid.

p. 18: [sidebar] "tall and muscular . . . giantess": Ibid.

p. 19: "Great indeed was his shame," and "thus worsted by a girl!": Ibid., p. 395

p. 19: "lively, tall, and good-looking.": Rashid, p. 309.

Maid in Armor: Joan of Arc

p. 22: We don't know much . . . eight inches tall: Pickels, pp. 30–31.

p. 22: She believed she saw some . . . Reims for his coronation: Pernoud and Clin, pp. 36–37.

p. 23: This meeting did not . . . persisted: Ibid., p. 18.

p. 23: She'd also cut her hair . . . "the Joan of Arc."): Harrison, p. 68.

p. 23: He sent word . . . and a cap: Ibid., p. 66.

p. 24: Joan was given a month-long . . . ride it. Ibid., pp. 72–73.

p. 24: Was this peasant girl . . . didn't show it: Pernoud and Clin, p. 23.

p. 24: She went straight . . . to save France: Pickels, pp. 28–29.

p. 24: made them go to confession . . . not to swear: Ibid., p. 35.

p. 25: [sidebar] By 1420 . . . taken a heavy toll: Brooks, pp. 7–9.

p. 27: Joan was ambushed . . . Burgundians: Pickels, p. 44.

p. 27: Another accusation . . . about wearing men's clothing: Garber, p. 216.

p. 27: "No. And even . . . before my capture!": quoted in Trask, p. 113.

The Chic of Araby:
Lady Mary Montagu

p. 29: illness that people feared . . . rest of their life: Rosenhek.

p. 29: "Poor Lady Mary . . . severely markt": James Brydges to Colonel Bladen, December 28, 1715, quoted in Sherburn, p. 208n.

p. 30: She visited the women's baths . . . she was a foreigner: Konuk, p. 393.

p. 30: "The first piece . . . silver flowers": Halsband, *Selected*, p. 95.

p. 30: She may also have started an art trend . . . veils and Turkish trousers: Konuk, p. 395; Garber, p. 312; Fischer, p. 116.

p. 31: "The smallpox, so fatal . . . they give it)": Halsband, *Selected*, p. 98.

p. 31: The procedure involved . . . than doing nothing: Last, p. 861.

p. 33: "You may believe . . . in England": Halsband, *Selected*, p. 99.

p. 33: Mary decided to have . . . surviving child variolated: Barnes, p. 330, p. 346.

p. 34: Many of Mary's friends . . . undergo the treatment: Rosenhek.

p. 35: Many members of the clergy . . . will of God: Halsband, "New Light," p. 399.

p. 35: "an Experiment . . . unthinking People": quoted in Barnes, p.349.

p. 35: The "ignorant women" jab . . . furious response: Halsband, "New Light," p. 400.

p. 35: "A Plain Account . . . Small Pox": Ibid.

p. 35: "I am determined . . . consequence whatever": quoted in Ibid.

p. 35: "I shall get nothing . . . good to mankind": quoted in Ibid.

Partners in Crime:
Anne Bonny and Mary Read

p. 38: Anne was born . . . pregnant with Anne: Duncombe, p. 122.

p. 38: "put into Breeches . . . be his Clerk": Johnson, p. 171.

p. 38: Anne helped run . . . James Bonny: Duncombe, pp. 122–23.

p. 38: "a young Fellow . . . worth a Groat": Johnson, p. 172.

p. 38: "in Men's Cloaths": Ibid.

p. 38: Like her . . . sailcloth: Duncombe, p. 168.

p. 38: Then one day . . . Mary Read: Ibid., p. 124.

p. 39: [sidebar] Captains were elected . . . share of the booty: Duncombe, p. 117.

p. 39: [sidebar] But pirating . . . or executed: Burl, chapter 5.

p. 40: "cut her new Lover's . . . Secret also": Johnson, p. 162.

p. 40: "Whether he was . . . returned more": Ibid., p. 157.

p. 40: "was obliged to put . . . as a Foot-boy": Ibid., p. 159.

p. 40: "a Vessel bound for the West-Indies": Ibid., p. 160.

p. 41: With the rest of the crew . . . captured: Duncombe, pp. 126–27.

p. 41: "Piracies . . . High Sea": Duncombe, p. 127; Stanley, p. 179.

p. 41: "wore Men's Jackets . . . Swore at the Men": Stanley, p. 179.

p. 41: "If he had fought . . . like a Dog": quoted in Johnson, p. 173.

p. 41: Court records . . . new disguise: Duncombe, pp. 128–29.

Bound and Determined:
Deborah Sampson

p. 44: Deborah was born . . . as indentured servants: Mann, pp. 45–46.

p. 44: For eight years . . . strong and lean; Taylor, p. 35.

p. 45: It turned out . . . in New York: Ibid., p. 35.

p. 45: "Officers in search . . . light infantry": Young, p. 98.

p. 46: Some sort of epidemic . . . deadly: Ibid., p. 149

p. 47: "a lively . . . undiscovered": *The Independent Gazette or the New-York Journal Revisited*, January 10, 1784, page 1.

p. 47: She petitioned . . . Hancock: Young, p.185; Mann, xvi–xvii.

Around the World in Three Thousand-and-Something Days: Jeanne Baret

p. 49: In 1766 the king . . . to be left behind: Ridley, p. 58.

p. 50: They collected . . . and physicians": Ibid., p. 16.

p. 50: Most university-trained . . . plants in the wild: Ibid., pp. 16–17.

p. 50: Commerson recognized . . . wouldn't seem suspicious: Ibid., p. 60.

p. 50: The other sailors on board . . . visible to everyone: Ibid., p. 78.

p. 51: She probably carried . . . butterfly net: Ibid., p. 101.

p. 51: One day when Commerson . . . the United States: Ibid., pp. 96–97.

p. 52: It's not entirely clear . . . of the Pacific Ocean: Bougainville, pp. 142–43.

p. 52: Some accounts say . . . was really Jeanne: Ridley, p. 2.

p. 52: Then, with a cordial . . . back to France: Bougainville, pp. 202–3.

p. 52: [sidebar] Pierre Poivre's name . . . had been "pickled": Maverick, p. 165; Ridley, p. 206.

p. 53: His specimens . . . shipped back to France: Ridley, p. 227.

Native Fighter: Running Eagle

p. 55: Running Eagle . . . them was chief: Hungry Wolf, p. 62.

p. 56: This is probably a reference . . . following buffalo: Lewis.

p. 57: One day while . . . around many a campfire: "Amazing Montanans," p. 33–34.

p. 58: [sidebar] More recently . . . many Indigenous cultures.: Roscoe, pp. 108–12, 178.

p. 58: [sidebar] When nineteenth-century Europeans . . . shocked and disapproving: Thayer, p. 288.

p. 59: Her fellow warriors . . . vision of the sun: McManus, pp. 384–85.

p. 59: That was usually . . . P'tamaka: McManus, pp. 384–85.

p. 59: It was an ancient . . . Braves Society: Hungry Wolf, p. 67.

p. 59: Her warrior uniform . . . war shield: Hungry Wolf, p. 67; Lang, p. 277.

p. 59: "No one needs . . . precious metals": *Montana Post*, December 9, 1865.

East Beats West: Lakshmibai

p. 61: "I will show you . . . my words!": quoted in Grewal, p. 57.

p. 62: After the marriage . . . her military training: Ibid., p. 56.

p. 66: "She used to dress . . . rode like one": quoted in Jerosch, p. 4.

p. 66: "extraordinary . . . forcefulness": Ibid., p. 56.

p. 66: "logical mind and potent intellect": Ibid.

p. 66: "an influential . . . adversary": Ibid., p. 3.

p. 66: Finally the British managed . . . in the opposite wall: Jerosch, pp. 202–3.

p. 67: Her followers carried . . . a mango tree: Ibid., p. 2.

p. 67: Just before she died . . . receive her jewelry: Ibid., p. 268.

p. 67: "Outstandingly she fought . . . Rani of Jhansi": Chauhan.

A Hostile Makeover: Amelia Bloomer

p. 69: In her essay . . . weight to lug around: Bloomer, Amelia Jenks.

p. 70: "is collecting the sweepings . . . the new dress": Bloomer, Amelia Jenks.

p. 72: "If the dress . . . abundant fruit": Bloomer, D. C., p. 70.

p. 73: When Elizabeth Cady Stanton's . . . bloomer outfit: Ginzberg, p. 82.

p. 73: And by the 1860s . . . short amount of time: Batterberry and Batterberry, p. 237.

p. 73: [sidebar] "The legal theory is . . . competence to perform": quoted in Gattey, p. 21.

p. 75: "charged with . . . male attire": "Girl Bicyclist."

p. 75: "a stiff shirt . . . a man's hat": Ibid.

p. 75: "The fashionable girl . . . and bloomers": *Chicago Post*, May 1897, quoted in Bushnell, p. 170.

p. 75: "Bicycle dresses. . . wear anywhere": "Bicycle Girls."

Leading the Way: Harriet Tubman

p. 77: Over ten years . . . nineteen trips: Jackson, p. 14

p. 77: She was often called . . . General Tubman: Gibson and Silverman, p. 29.

p. 77: "one of the bravest persons on this continent": quoted in Clinton, *Road*, p. 26.

p. 77: "the most of a man . . . ever met with": Ibid.

p. 78: During the war . . . network of agents: Gibson and Silverman, p. 26.

p. 78: Perhaps her greatest . . . attacked the plantations: Clinton, "General."

p. 78: In the process . . . ships and freedom: Jackson, p. 44.

p. 78: "The enemy seems . . . river and country": quoted in Jackson, p. 44.

p. 78: "tore it almost off . . . else but shreds": quoted in Humez, p. 60.

p. 78: "a bloomer dress . . . wear on expeditions": Ibid.

p. 81: On cloudy nights . . . side of the trunk: Jackson, p. 13.

p. 81: [sidebar] Because wanted posters . . . herself as a man: Gibson and Silverman, p. 31.

p. 82: On her third trip . . . group safely north: Jackson, p. 13.

p. 83: A woman named Sarah . . . a small pension: Gibson and Silverman, p. 27.

Skirting the Issue: Rosa Bonheur

p. 85: The law allowed . . . necessary.: "Frenchwomen in Trousers."

p. 85: The only time . . . during Carnival: Van Slyke, "Sexual," p. 321.

p. 85: A woman who dressed . . . likely a harlot: Van Slyke, "War," p. 40.

p. 86: "I wed art . . . the air I breathe": Klumpke, p. xviii.

p. 86: "prematurely worn out . . . a precarious life": quoted in Stanton, p. 9.

p. 87: "Mother of three boys . . . was called Eleanor": Ibid., p. 11.

p. 87: "grotesque figures . . . of the principal": Ibid., p. 36.

p. 87: "I ordered . . . was her pride": Ibid., p. 11.

p. 88: Every day Rosa's brother . . . stairs to graze: Stanton, p. 37.

p. 88: She spent long days . . . horses, and oxen: Ibid., p 21.

p. 88: She also kept a pistol in her pocket: Van Slyke, "Sexual," p. 328.

p. 90: "dress as a man" and "health reasons": quoted in Mesch.

p. 90: "shows, balls, . . . to the public": Ibid.

p. 90: "divided skirts" and "holds in her hand . . . reins of a horse": quoted in Gibson, Megan.

p. 91: [sidebar] Early in her career . . . for her writing: Jack, p. 162.

p. 91: [sidebar] "No one knew me . . . stopped me": quoted in Jack, p. 163.

p. 91: [sidebar] "What the deuce . . . gad about!": quoted in Stanton, p. 38.

Frocks and Bonds: Ellen Craft

p. 93: The young man's . . . eyes: Craft, p. 35; Garber, p. 284.

p. 93: "a very fine morning": Craft, p. 44.

p. 93: "I will make him hear!" and "It is a very fine morning sir!": Ibid.

p. 93: "not trouble that fellow any more": Ibid.

p. 98: "Thank God . . . safe": Ibid, p. 79.

p. 99: Abolitionists encouraged . . . their arrest: Sterling, p. 23.

No Reservations: Lozen

p. 101: Victorio was the leader . . . for three years: Aleshire, p. 11; "Plateaus and Canyonlands: Apache."

p. 101: Next to Lozen . . . named Eclode: Aleshire, p. 12.

p. 101: According to oral . . . enemy's location: Ball, Henn, and Sanchez, p. 62.

p. 102: "Lozen is as my right hand" and "Strong as . . . to her people": quoted in Sonneborn and in Docevski.

p. 102: "No man in the tribe . . . stampeding a herd": quoted in Robinson.

p. 102: "Killing a longhorn . . . to their retreat": Ball, p. 116.

p. 102: From where she hid . . . range of the bullets: Ibid., p. 117.

p. 103: As they traveled . . . Eclode's people safely: Aleshire, p. 268.

p. 103: The news . . . 160 in number: Moore, p. 102.

p. 104: The captives were . . . sold into slavery: Ibid.

p. 104: She immediately set off . . . to get away: Rangel.

p. 104: Meanwhile, the Apache leader . . . Mexican settlements: Cassidy, Walker, and Maynard, pp. 322–23.

p. 104: By 1886 Geronimo . . . three thousand Mexican troops: Stockel, pp. 48–49.

p. 104: So he sent Lozen . . . a truce: Ibid., p. 31.

p. 104: It was then that they learned . . . agreed to surrender: Cassidy, Walker, and Maynard, pp. 323–24.

p. 105: [sidebar] The living conditions . . . killed many people: Cassidy, Walker, and Maynard, p. 320.

p. 105: [sidebar] "They knew the trails . . . place of business": "Into the Apache's Lair."

p. 105: [sidebar] "They . . . 'double-quick' time": "Indians in the Army."

p. 105: [sidebar] "The mountain . . . forty miles a day." John A. Glass quoted in "In Pursuit of Victorio's Band."

For She's a Jolly Good Fellow: Vesta Tilley

p. 110: "I felt that I could . . . dressed as a boy": "Vesta Tilly."

p. 112: Vesta came of age . . . 1860 to 1920: Maitland, p. 11.

p. 114: Nevertheless . . . performing: Ibid., p. 30

Winging It: Lilian Bland

p. 117: She built it using . . . aunt's ear trumpet: *Encyclopedia of World Biography*, "Lilian Bland."

p. 118: The prim-and-proper . . . and fixed up cars: Ibid.

p. 119: It was from birds . . . lift and drag: Ibid.

p. 119: [sidebar] At the time Lilian . . . tough story to verify: McCullough, p. 204.

p. 121: Lilian's was made . . . crisscrossing wires: *Encyclopedia of World Biography*, "Lilian Bland."

p. 121: She persuaded . . . the ropes: McIlwaine.

p. 121: "If it gets annoyed . . . inducement to fly!": quoted in Warner.

p. 122: "I find mechanic's . . . thing to wear" and "Skirts are out . . . speak of oil": Bland.

p. 122: [sidebar] How to Start Up a Model T . . . : "How To: Drive a Ford Model T."

Viva La Frida: Frida Kahlo

p. 125: Frida Kahlo was always . . . all the time: "Frida Kahlo, Appearances Can Be Deceiving."

p. 126: Frida lay in the street . . . ribs were broken: Herrera, p. 49.

p. 126: She spent most of . . . growing enthusiasm: Grimberg, p. 15.

p. 126: "I'm still alive . . . something is painting": quoted in Souter, p. 23.

p. 126: Her mother . . . ancestry: Grimberg, p. 9.

p. 126: As a kid she often . . . her legs' lengths: Ibid., p. 12.

p. 127: Frida attended . . . excellent student: Herrera, p. 27.

p. 128: Frida's mother likened . . . elephant and a dove: Udall, p. 13.

p. 128: "Wife of the Master . . . Works of Art": Davies.

p. 128: "Of course he . . . the big artist": quoted in Davies.

p. 128: Other times she showed . . . festooned it with flowers: Prignitz-Poda, p. 31.

p. 128: [sidebar] Whether she liked it . . . surrealists: Prignitz-Poda, p. 46.

p. 128: [sidebar] "They thought I was . . . my own reality": quoted in Márquez, p. 92.

p. 130: "There have been two . . . far the worst": quoted in Herrera, p. 107.

Playing Hardball: Marcenia "Toni" Stone

p. 133: Father Keefe agreed to . . . couldn't give up baseball: Davis, p. 76; Ackmann, p. 2.

p. 133: She was good at . . . tennis, and skating: Ackmann, p. xi.

p. 133: Somehow Father Keefe . . . teams in the city: Ibid., p. 40.

p. 134: "I took it home . . . give up baseball": quoted in Hayes.

p. 134: The Black barnstorming . . . Negro leagues: Ackmann, p. 49.

p. 136: One day Toni met . . . drove in two runs: Davis, p. 78.

p. 137: "He was out": quoted in Thomas.

p. 137: 'Hey, T! . . . hurt me'": Ibid.

p. 137: "It was a lulu": Ibid.

p. 139: [sidebar] Around the same time . . . wasn't serious baseball: Shattuck, p. 65.

p. 139: [sidebar] Team owners told . . . around at the plate: Ibid., p. 74.

p. 139: [sidebar] Female college baseball . . . to first base: Gregorich, p. 3.

p. 139: [sidebar] players wore short . . . with the press: Heaphy, pp. 252–53.

The Most Riveting Riveter: Marguerite Johnson

p. 142: "I saw women . . . form-fitting jackets": "How Dr. Maya Angelou Became San Francisco's First Black Streetcar Conductor."

p. 142: "I sat [there] . . . I got the job": Ibid.

p. 143: After divorcing one . . . her professional name: Angelou, p. 127.

p. 144: [sidebar] In 1943 twenty-two . . . in their department: Ryon; Honey, p. 37.

p. 145: "Absolutely not . . . 'I'll start tomorrow'": quoted in Fox.

p. 145: "a brilliant writer . . . phenomenal woman": Ibid.

Author's Note

p. 147: [sidebar] lest they . . . uterus: Verbrugge, p. 53.

Select Bibliography

Ackmann, Martha. *Curveball: The Remarkable Story of Toni Stone, the First Woman to Play Professional Baseball in the Negro League*. Chicago: Lawrence Hill Books, 2010.

Aleshire, Peter. *Warrior Woman: The Story of Lozen, Apache Warrior and Shaman*. New York: St. Martin's, 2001.

"Amazing Montanans." Montana Historical Society website.

Angelou, Maya. *Mom & Me & Mom*. London: Virago, 2014.

Ball, Eve. *In the Days of Victorio: Recollections of a Warm Springs Apache*. Tucson: University of Arizona Press, 1997.

———, with Nora Henn and Lynda Sanchez. *Indeh, an Apache Odyssey*. Provo, UT: Brigham Young University Press, 1980.

Barnes, Diana. "The Public Life of a Woman of Wit and Quality: Lady Mary Wortley Montagu and the Vogue for Smallpox Inoculation." *Feminist Studies* 38, no. 2 (Summer 2012): 330–62.

Batterberry, Michael, and Ariane Batterberry. *Fashion, the Mirror of History*. New York: Chanticleer, 1977.

"Bicycle Girls and their Summer Road Gowns." *San Francisco Call*, May 29, 1898.

Bland, Lilian. "The 'Mayfly': The First Irish Biplane and How She Was Built." *Flight* 2, no. 51 (December 17, 1910): 1025–27.

Bloomer, Amelia Jenks. "The New Costume for the Ladies." *The Lily*, September 1, 1851.

Bloomer, D. C. *The Life and Writings of Amelia Bloomer.* Boston: Arena, 1895.

Bougainville, Louis-Antoine de. A *Voyage Round the World*. Translated by John Reinhold Forster. Cambridge: Cambridge University Press, 2011. First published 1772 by J. Nourse, London.

Brooks, Polly Schoyer. *Beyond the Myth: The Story of Joan of Arc*. New York: JB Lippincott, 1990.

Burl, Aubrey. *Black Barty: Bartholomew Roberts and His Pirate Crew 1718–1723*. Stroud, England: Sutton, 2006.

Bushnell, George D. "When Chicago Was Wheel Crazy." *Chicago History* 4, no. 3 (Fall 1975): 67–75.

Cassidy, James, Chief Bryce Walker, and Jill Maynard, eds. *Through Indian Eyes: The Untold Story of Native American Peoples*. Pleasantville, NY: Reader's Digest, 1995.

Chauhan, Subhadra Kumari. "Jhansi ki Rani." Translated by Nandini Bajpai for the author.

Clinton, Catherine. "'General Tubman': Female Abolitionist Was Also a Secret Military Weapon." *Military Times*, February 6, 2018.

———. *The Road to Freedom*. New York: Little, Brown, 2004.

Clough, A. H. *Plutarch's Lives: The Translation Called Dryden's, Corrected from the Greek and Revised*. Vol. 4. Boston: Little, Brown, 1905.

Cohen, Jennie. "Did Skin Cream Kill Egypt's Queen Hatshepsut?" History.com, August 29, 2008.

Craft, William. *Running a Thousand Miles for Freedom*. University of Virginia Library; NetLibrary, 2001. First published 1860 by William Tweedie, London.

Cretaz, Britni de la. "Androgyny Is Now Fashionable in the W.N.B.A." *New York Times*, June 18, 2019.

Davies, Florence. "Wife of the Master Mural Painter Gleefully Dabbles in Works of Art." *Detroit News*, February 2, 1933.

Davis, Amira Rose. "No League of Their Own." *Radical History Review*, no. 125 (2016): 74–96.

Davison, Michael Worth, and Neal V. Martin, eds. *Everyday Life Through the Ages*. London: Reader's Digest, 1992.

Docevski, Boban. "The 'Apache Joan of Arc' and the Other Courageous Native American Women of the 19th Century." *Vintage News*, March 12, 2018.

Duncombe, Laura Sook. *Pirate Women: The Princesses, Prostitutes, and Privateers Who Ruled the Seven Seas*. Chicago: Chicago Review Press, 2017.

Encyclopedia of World Biography Online. "Lilian Bland." Detroit: Gale, 2017.

Fischer, Gayle V. "'Pantalets' and 'Turkish Trowsers': Designing Freedom in the Mid-Nineteenth-Century United States." *Feminist Studies* 23, no. 1 (Spring 1997): 110–40.

Flam, Lisa. "Pennsylvania Girl Says Suit Kept Her Out of Prom: 'I Felt Really Beautiful.'" *Today Show* website, May 11, 2016.

Fox, Margalit. "Maya Angelou, Lyrical Witness of the Jim Crow South, Dies at 86." *New York Times*, May 28, 2014.

Frantz, Donald G. *Blackfoot Grammar*, 3rd ed. Toronto: University of Toronto Press, 2017.

"Frenchwomen in Trousers." *Colusa (CA) Daily Sun*, October 18, 1893.

"Frida Kahlo: Appearances Can Be Deceiving." Brooklyn Museum, exhibit description.

"Frida Kahlo, Artist, Diego Rivera's Wife." *New York Times*, July 14, 1954.

Garber, Marjorie B. *Vested Interests: Cross-Dressing & Cultural Anxiety*. New York: Routledge, 1997.

Gattey, Charles Neilson. *The Bloomer Girls*. New York: Coward-McCann, 1968.

Gibson, Chantal N., and Monique Silverman. "Sur/Rendering Her Image: The Unknowable Harriet Tubman." *Canadian Art Review* 30, no. 1/2 (2005): 25–38.

Gibson, Megan. "It Is Now Legal for Women to Wear Pants in Paris." *Time*, February 4, 2013.

Ginzberg, Lori D. *Elizabeth Cady Stanton: An American Life*. New York: Hill and Wang, 2009.

"Girl Bicyclist in Trouble." *New York Times*, July 2, 1898: 7.

Glass, John A. as quoted in "In Pursuit of Victorio's Band: A Cavalry Lieutenant's Narrative of a Stern Chase in the Indian War of 1879." *Wood County Reporter*, February 22, 1890.

Gregorich, Barbara. *Women at Play: The Story of Women in Baseball*. San Diego: Harcourt Brace, 1993.

Grewal, Jyoti. "Lakshmibai." In *Women in World History: A Biographical Encyclopedia*, vol. 9, edited by Anne Commire. Durham, NC: Duke University Press/Yorkin Publications, 2001.

Grimberg, Salomon. *Frida Kahlo*. North Dighton, MA: JG Press, 1997.

Halsband, Robert. "New Light on Lady Mary Wortley Montagu's Contribution to Inoculation." *Journal of the History of Medicine and Allied Sciences* 8, no. 4 (October 1953): 390–405.

———, ed. *The Selected Letters of Lady Mary Wortley Montagu*. New York: St. Martin's, 1970.

Harrison, Kathryn. *Joan of Arc: A Life Transfigured*. New York: Doubleday, 2014.

Hayes, Bob. "To This Ms., Diamond Is Made of Dirt." *San Francisco Examiner*, May 4, 1976.

Heaphy, Lesley. "Women Playing Hardball." In *Baseball and Philosophy: Thinking Outside the Batter's Box*, edited by Eric Bronson. Chicago: Open Court, 2004.

Herrera, Hayden. *Frida: A Biography of Frida Kahlo*. New York: Harper and Row, 1983.

Honey, Maureen, ed. *Bitter Fruit: African American Women in World War II*. Columbia: University of Missouri Press, 1999.

"How Dr. Maya Angelou Became San Francisco's First Black Streetcar Conductor." *Super Soul Sunday*, episode 410, OWN Network, May 12, 2013.

"How To: Drive a Ford Model T." *Car and Driver*, July 1, 2009.

Humez, Jean McMahon. *Harriet Tubman: The Life and the Life Stories*. Madison: University of Wisconsin Press, 2003.

Hungry Wolf, Beverly. *The Ways of My Grandmothers*. New York: Quill, 1982.

"Indians in the Army." *Lola (KS) Register*, November 9, 1894.

"In Pursuit of Victorio's Band: A Cavalry Lieutenant's Narrative of a Stern Chase in the Indian War of 1879." *Wood County (WI) Reporter*, February 22, 1890.

"Into the Apache's Lair." *Barton County (KS) Democrat*, March 4, 1897.

Jack, Belinda Elizabeth. *George Sand: A Woman's Life Writ Large*. London: Vintage, 2001.

Jackson, George F. *Black Women, Makers of History: A Portrait*. Santa Rosa, CA: Distributed by National Women's History Project, 1985.

Jerosch, Rainer. *The Rani of Jhansi: Rebel Against Will: A Biography of the Legendary Indian Freedom Fighter in the Mutiny of 1857–1858*. Translated by James A. Turner. Delhi: Aakar, 2007.

Johnson, Charles. *A General History of the Pyrates*. London: Charles Rivington, 1724.

Keller, Cathleen A. "Hatshepsut's Reputation in History." In *Hatshepsut: From Queen to Pharaoh*, edited by Catharine H. Roehrig. New York: Metropolitan Museum of Art, 2005.

Klumpke, Anna. *Rosa Bonheur: The Artist's (Auto)biography*. Translated by Gretchen van Slyke. Ann Arbor: The University of Michigan Press, 2001.

Konuk, Kader. "Ethnomasquerade in Ottoman-European Encounters: Reenacting Lady Mary Wortley Montagu." *Criticism* 46, no. 3. Detroit: Wayne State University Press, 2004.

Krippes, Karl A. "Wrestling and Wrestler as Epic Aspects of the 'Secret History.'" *Mongolian Studies* 12 (1989): 95–100.

Lang, Sabine. *Men as Women, Women as Men: Changing Gender in Native American Cultures*. Austin: University of Texas Press, 1998.

Last, John M. "Vaccination." In *Encyclopedia of Children and Childhood, in History and Society*, vol. 3, edited by Paula S. Fass. New York: Macmillan Reference, 2004.

Lewis, Orrin. "Blackfoot Indian Fact Sheet." *Native Languages of the Americas*, www.bigorrin.org/blackfoot_kids.htm.

Maglaty, Jeanne. "When Did Girls Start Wearing Pink?" Smithsonian website, April 7, 2011.

Maitland, Sara. *Vesta Tilley 1864–1952*. London: Virago, 1986.

Mann, Herman. "Life of Deborah Sampson: The Female Soldier in the War of the Revolution." *The Female Review*, edited by John Adams Vinton. Boston: J. K. Wiggin and W. P. Lunt, 1797.

Márquez, F. "Art: Mexican Autobiography." *Time*, April 27, 1953: 92.

Maverick, Lewis A. "Pierre Poivre: Eighteenth Century Explorer of Southeast Asia." *Pacific Historical Review* 10, no. 2 (June 1941): 165–77.

Mayor, Adrienne. *The Amazons: Lives and Legends of Warrior Women Across the Ancient World*. Princeton, NJ: Princeton University Press, 2014.

———. *The Poison King: The Life and Legend of Mithradates, Rome's Deadliest Enemy*. Princeton, NJ: Princeton University Press, 2010.

McCullough, David. *The Wright Brothers: The Dramatic Story Behind the Legend*. New York: Simon & Schuster, 2016.

McIlwaine, Eddie. "Journalist, Photographer, Crackshot and the First Woman to Fly an Aeroplane . . . the Amazing Lilian Bland." *Belfast Telegraph*, August 13, 2010.

McManus, Sheila. "Pi'tamakan." In *Encyclopedia of Lesbian, Gay, Bisexual and Transgender History in America*, vol. 2, edited by Marc Stein. New York: Scribner's, 2004.

Mesch, Rachel. "Clothes Make the (Wo)man? Pants Permits in Nineteenth-Century Paris." *Wonders and Marvels* (blog), September 2, 2015.

Moore, Laura Jane. "Lozen: An Apache Woman Warrior." In *Sifters: Native American Women's Lives*, edited by Theda Perdue. Oxford: Oxford University Press, 2001.

Pernoud, Régine, and Marie-Véronique Clin. *Joan of Arc: Her Story*. Translated by Jeremy DuQuesnay Adams. New York: St. Martin's, 1998.

Pickels, Dwayne E. *Joan of Arc*. Philadelphia: Chelsea House, 2002.

"Plateaus and Canyonlands: Apache." Texas Beyond History website.

Prignitz-Poda, Helga. *Frida Kahlo: The Painter and Her Work*. Munich: Schirmer/Mosel, 2004.

Rangel, Valerie. "The Story of Lozen." NewMexicoHistory.org. Office of the State Historian, New Mexico.

Rashīd al-Dīn, Tabīb. *Rashiduddin Fazlullah's Jami'u't-Tawarikh/Compendium of Chronicles: A History of the Mongols*, edited by W. M. Thackston. Cambridge, MA: Harvard University Press, 1999. Originally published in the early fifteenth century by the Padishah of Islam Oljaitii Sultan, in the name of his brother Sultan Sa'id Ghazan Khan, Anatolia.

Rediker, Marcus. "When Women Pirates Sailed the Seas." *Wilson Quarterly* 17, no. 4 (Autumn 1993): 102–10.

Ridley, Glynis. *The Discovery of Jeanne Baret: A Story of Science, the High Seas, and the First Woman to Circumnavigate the Globe*. New York: Crown, 2010.

Robinson, Sherry. "Lozen: Apache Woman Warrior." *Wild West* 10, no. 1 (1997).

Roehrig, Catharine H., Renee Dreyfus, and Cathleen A. Keller. Introduction to *Hatshepsut: From Queen to Pharaoh*, edited by Catharine H. Roehrig. New York: Metropolitan Museum of Art, 2005.

Roscoe, Will. *Changing Ones: Third and Fourth Genders in Native North America*. New York: St. Martin's, 1998.

Rosenhek, Jackie. "Safe Smallpox Inoculations." *Doctor's Review, Medicine on the Move*, Feb. 2005.

Roth, Ann Macy. "Models of Authority." In *Hatshepsut: From Queen to Pharaoh*, edited by Catharine H. Roehrig, New York: Metropolitan Museum of Art, 2005.

Ryon, Roderick. "When Baltimore's War Effort Tripped Over Race." *Baltimore Sun*, August 11, 1993.

Shattuck, Debra A. *Bloomer Girls: Women Baseball Pioneers*. Urbana: University of Illinois Press, 2017.

Sherburn, George. *The Early Career of Alexander Pope*. Oxford: Clarendon, 1934.

Sonneborn, Liz. *A to Z of American Indian Women*. New York: Facts on File, 2007.

Souter, Gary. *Frida Kahlo: 1907–1954*. New York: Parkstone, 2011.

Stanley, Jo. *Bold in Her Breeches: Women Pirates Across the Ages*. London: Pandora, 1996.

Stanton, Theodore, ed. *Reminiscences of Rosa Bonheur*. New York: Hacker Art Books, 1976. First published in 1910 by Andrew Melrose, London.

Sterling, Dorothy. *Black Foremothers: Three Lives*. New York: Feminist Press, 1988.

Stockel, H. Henrietta. *Women of the Apache Nation: Voices of Truth*. Reno: University of Nevada Press, 1991.

Taylor, Alan. "Transformer." *New Republic* 230, no. 23 (2004): 32–37.

Thayer, James Steel. "The Berdache of the Northern Plains: A Socioreligious Perspective." *Journal of Anthropological Research* 36, no. 3 (Autumn 1980): 287–93.

Thomas, Robert McG. Jr. "Toni Stone, 75, First Woman to Play Big-League Baseball." *New York Times,* November 10, 1996.

Trask, Willard, trans. *Joan of Arc in Her Own Words.* New York: Turtle Point, 1996.

Udall, Sharyn R. "Frida Kahlo's Mexican Body: History, Identity, and Artistic Aspiration." *Woman's Art Journal* 24, no. 2 (Autumn 2003): 10–14.

Van Slyke, Gretchen. "The Sexual and Textural Politics of Dress: Rosa Bonheur and Her Cross-Dressing Permits." *Nineteenth-Century French Studies* 26, no. 3/4 (Spring–Summer 1998): 321–35.

———. "Women at War: Skirting the Issue in the French Revolution." *L'Esprit Créateur* 37, no. 1 (Spring 1997): 33–43.

Verbrugge, Martha H. "Gender, Science & Fitness: Perspectives on Women's Exercise in the United States in the 20th Century." *Health and History* 4, no. 1 (2002): 52–72.

"Vesta Tilley." Victoria and Albert Museum website.

Warner, Guy. "Lilian Bland Lecture." Ulster Museum, April 7, 2018.

Weatherford, Jack. *The Secret History of the Mongol Queens: How the Daughters of Genghis Khan Rescued His Empire.* New York: Crown, 2010.

———. "The Wrestler Princess." *Lapham's Quarterly,* September 27, 2010.

Wilford, John Noble. "Tooth May Have Solved Mummy Mystery." *New York Times,* June 27, 2007.

Worrall, Simon. "Amazon Warriors Did Indeed Fight and Die Like Men." *National Geographic,* October 28, 2014.

Young, Alfred Fabian. *Masquerade: The Life and Times of Deborah Sampson, Continental Soldier.* New York: Knopf, 2004.

Yule, Henry, ed. *The Book of Ser Marco Polo, the Venetian, Concerning the Kingdoms and Marvels of the East,* vol. 2. London: John Murray, 1875.

Zinko, Carolyne. "A Day in the Life of . . . Nan Kempner: She'll take Manhattan—but she misses San Francisco." *SFGate,* July 11, 2004.

Image Credits

p. viii: *Young Boy with Whip,* artist unknown, ca. 1840 / Wikimedia Commons

p. x: *Portrait of Two Boys,* artist unknown, ca. 1600 / Wikimedia Commons

p. 4: *Large Kneeling Statue of Hatshepsut,* artist unknown, ca. 1479–1458 BCE / Metropolitan Museum of Art, Rogers Fund

p. 6: *The Mortuary Temple of Hatshepsut,* Hesham Ebaid, 2016 / Wikimedia Commons

p. 12: Vase with Amazon wearing trousers, ca 470 BCE, photo by Marie-Lan Nguyen / British Museum / Wikimedia Commons

p. 16: Painting of Shizu [Kublai Khan], Anige of Nepal, ca. 1294 / Wikimedia Commons

p. 18: *Qutulun, Daughter of Qaidu,* Maître de la Mazarine, ca. 1410 / Wikimedia Commons

p. 23: *Joan of Arc,* artist and date unknown, Archives Nationales (France) / Wikimedia Commons

p. 25: *Bataille d'Azincourt (1415)*, artist unknown, ca. 1484 / Wikimedia Commons

p. 26: *Joan of Arc Is Interrogated by the Cardinal of Winchester in Her Prison*, Hippolyte Delaroche, 1824 / Musée des Beaux-Arts, Rouen, France / Wikimedia Commons

p. 31: *Smallpox, textured illustration, Japanese manuscript*, Kanda Gensen, ca. 1720 / Wellcome Library, London / Wellcome Images

p. 32: *Pope Makes Love to Lady Mary Wortley Montagu*, William Powell Frith, 1852 / Auckland Art Gallery / Wikimedia Commons

p. 34: *The Public Vaccinator*, Lance Calkin, ca. 1901 / Wellcome Library, London / Wellcome Images

p. 39: Anne Bonny & Mary Read, Benjamin Cole, from *A General History of the Robberies and Murders of the Most Notorious Pyrates*, 1724 / www.archive.org

p. 45: Deborah Sampson, artist unknown, from *The Female Review; or Life of Deborah Sampson*, 1797 / www.archive.org

p. 51: Color drawing of Bougainvillea, Lena Lowis, 1878 / Wikimedia Commons

p. 52: *Mad_lla Bare*, artist unknown, from *Navigazioni Di Cook Pel Grande Oceano e Intorno Al Globo. Sonzogno e Comp.*, 1816 / The Mitchell Library, The State Library of New South Wales

p. 56: *Stu-mick-o-súcks, Buffalo Bull's Back Fat, Head Chief*, 1832, George Catlin / Smithsonian American Art Museum, gift of Mrs. Joseph Harrison, Jr.

p. 63: *27th Regiment of Madras Native Infantry*, Major Henry Bevan, from *Thirty Years in India: or, a Soldier's reminiscences of Native and European life in the Presidencies, from 1808 to 1838*, 1839 / Wikimedia Commons

p. 65: Lakshmibai, CPA Media Pte Ltd / Alamy Stock Photo

p. 71: *Group Portrait of Four Women, Two Men and Three Children in a Garden*, Franz Antoine, ca. 1850s–60s / Metropolitan Museum of Art, David Hunter McAlpin Fund, 1948

p. 72: *The New Woman—Wash Day*, Strohmeyer & Wyman, ca. 1897 / Library of Congress Prints and Photographs Division

p. 74 (top): *The Bicycle—the great dress reformer of the nineteenth century!*, S. D. Ehrhart, 1895 / Library of Congress Prints and Photographs Division

p. 74 (bottom): *The "New Woman" and Her Bicycle—there will be several varieties of her*, F. Opper, 1895 / Library of Congress Prints and Photographs Division

p. 79: *Raid of Second South Carolina Volunteers (Col. Montgomery) Among the Rice Plantations of the Combahee, S.C.*, Surgeon Robinson, *Harper's Weekly*, July 4, 1863 / www.archive.org

p. 80: *Portrait of Harriet Tubman*, Benjamin Powelson, 1868 or 1869 / Collection of the Library of Congress and the Smithsonian National Museum of African American History & Culture

p. 82: Runaway notice, *Cambridge Democrat*, 1849 / Wikimedia Commons

p. 83: *Johnson's Delaware and Maryland*, Alvin Jewett Johnson, 1864 / Wikimedia Commons

p. 87: *Plowing in the Nivernais*, Rosa Bonheur, 1849 / Wikimedia Commons

p. 89: *Rosa Bonheur*, André Adolphe-Eugène Disdéri, 1861–64 / The J. Paul Getty Museum, Los Angeles

p. 91: *Portrait of George Sand*, Nadar, 1864 / Wikimedia Commons

p. 95: Ellen Craft, S. S. Schoff, from *Running a Thousand Miles for Freedom*, 1860 / www.archive.org

p. 97: The Fugitive Slave Bill, 1854 / Collection of the Smithsonian National Museum of African American History and Culture

p. 98: Ellen and William Craft, artist unknown, from *The Underground Rail Road*, 1872 / www.archive.org

p. 105: *Apache Braves*, William Stinson Soule, 1869–74 / The J. Paul Getty Museum, Los Angeles

p. 106: *Jicarella Apache . . . Lately wedded*, Timothy H. O'Sullivan, 1874 / The J. Paul Getty Museum, Los Angeles

p. 111: *Vesta Tilley's Great Songs*, 1893 / Music Division, The New York Public Library Digital Collections

Index

Page numbers in *italics* indicate images.